*A Psychological Journey Toward
Befriending Yourself*

WHISPERS OF THE HEART

DALE R. OLEN PH.D.

Resource Publications, Inc.
160 E. Virginia St. #290
San Jose, CA 95112

TABLE OF CONTENTS

To Joelyn
whose heart whispers
the same word as mine

INTRODUCTION

If you see with your ears, feel, taste and smell with your ears, you will hear a cacophony of voices. These voices surround us. They ring in from all sides. They invade our spirits and babble to us in every language of Babel.

All the elements of the world — our cultures, our mores, our societal and religious formation — speak to us in every pitch and timbre imaginable. Oftentimes these voices shout to us, directing our lives like a dictator might his subjects.

But if we breathe deeply, slow down and listen intently, we may hear among the noise a faint whisper. From deep within the cavity of our hearts, a small voice beckons. It speaks a language we naturally understand, but may not recognize for lack of use. The voice never discourages, but continues day after day to speak in a gentle and quiet ways.

The message of this whisper stands as the central fact of human existence. If the voice were a teacher, it would state accurately: "Listen well, for this is your most important subject ever."

Although we know instinctively the language of our heart, many of us have un-learned its vocabulary and no longer recognize it. This book re-teaches, not only the heart's language, but the way to learn it again.

The fundamental principle framing the pursuit of our heart's whisper is: *We give power to whatever we focus on.* The way to the heart lies in our effort to "dis-

attend" to all the voices around us, and to attend to the
whisper within us. All of us know how to de-focus and re-
focus outside voices. When I read the newspaper (focus
on it) my wife tells me she has learned not to talk to me at
that time. (I de-focus her and my children's voices.)
While working on the jigsaw puzzle (focusing), we lose
track of time and say, "Gee, you mean I've been working
on this for two hours already. It seems like I just started."
We de-focus time. We receive our yearly work evalua-
tion and have nine very positive scores and one negative
score. We get upset because we focus on the single negative score and de-focus the nine positive scores.

Generally, most of us have learned to de-focus the
voice of our heart, and attend, instead, to all the voices of
the outer world. We listen to the media, the politicians,
the churches, all the teachers, our friends, parents and
relatives. But what of the voice within? We begin to gain
access to this voice by seeking it, by attempting to focus
on it, by listening closely.

But how do we focus on this inner voice that seems
so vital to our live? This book will take you on the journey of the heart teaching you a way to de-focus the outside voices and attend faithfully to your own inner voice.
The journey carries some pain, but mostly, surprise and
joy as well.

The U-Shaped Journey

The letter U describes the shape of the psychological
journey to our hearts (See figure 1). You will start at the
top left hand side of the U, move deeply within yourself,
touch your inner being and return to the exterior of your
life on the other side of the U.

At the top left hand side of the U you discover your
feelings and behaviors. These are the elements that express you to the outside world. As you begin to go down
the U line you have a variety of layers, which represent
the learned experiences and beliefs of your history. At
the bottom of the U lies your real self, made up of very

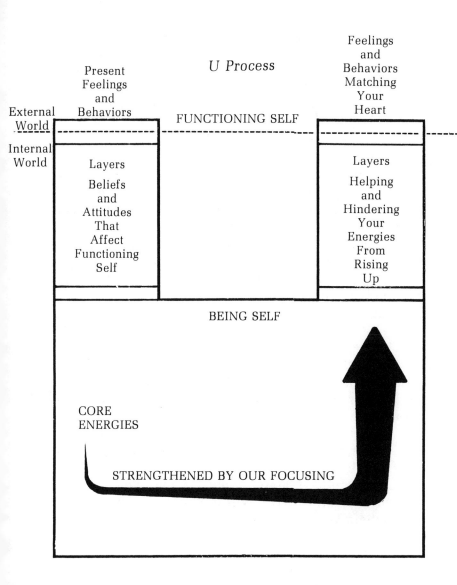

active and powerful energies. It is these energies that
you will want to discover and learn to activate. These
energies are the voice that whispers.

Once you immerse yourself in this voice and give
strength to your energies, they will begin to rise up the
other side of the U. Once again you will encounter layers
of beliefs and attitudes, some of which will facilitate
these energies in coming up directly, and others, which
will retard the energies from surfacing. At the top of the
U on the right hand side you will find those feelings and
behaviors that authentically express the energies found
at the bottom of your U.

So the psychological journey starts from your feelings and your behaviors as they exist presently, down
through the layers of your experience to the voice of your
heart. Then the movement proceeds from the core of
your being back up through layers of beliefs to the outside of yourself in feelings and behaviors that more
genuinely match the voice of your inner self. When your
feelings and behaviors authentically match this voice,
then you are true to yourself and at peace. Your outside
matches your inside. That is the key to mental health.

To begin this process, then, you will attending to
your present feelings and behavior. The journey inward
can only proceed if you can experience, know, and label
your feelings. Your ability to be in touch with your feelings through observation is your first task. It will be important for you to break down any defenses you might
have to allowing your feelings space and expression.

Once you have hold of your feelings, you can begin
the journey inward. You will then explore the attitudes
and beliefs you have that have created those feelings.
You will enter your many layers, some of which lead you
to life and other which lead you to death. You will be
asked to investigate all those layers, reinforcing the life-
giving ones and challenging and changing the sabatoging
ones. Some of those layers will serve as road blocks in
the journey to your heart. Those, especially, you will
want to knock out.

During this journey, I will share with you some ways of getting through those layers. We will use your feelings and behaviors as signals of your heart's voice, and work our way through your layers to reach the richness of your core self. Our efforts will be to reach your heart, your inner goodness, and to learn how to give it power and strength so that you can live according to the law of your heart rather than any external forces that attempt to dictate how you must function.

Once you touch your inner core, your work will be to keep yourself there. If you are like most people I work with, including myself, you will be tempted to change your U-shaped process into a V-shaped journey. That is, you might hear, momentarily, your inner voice, and then try to jump right back to the top of yourself with your feelings and behavior. I invite you to attempt remaining close to your heart. Simply touching it does not help. You need to dwell in your inner energies so they come alive in you.

When you spend time with your own voice, you have a much better chance of befriending yourself and liking who you are. *For you are your heart's whisper.* You are not your outer self, your feelings or your behavior; you are not your layers of thoughts and attitudes. No, *you are your heart.* And you give yourself power by focusing on those heart-energies.

The more you enter your heart and stay there, the more power you give those energies. And then, they will begin rising up the other side of your U. In the last part of this book we will identify those skills that best express the voice of your heart. The closer you live to your heart, the more likely you will experience yourself using, effectively, your ability to communicate, to believe reasonably, to engage the situations of your life, to act with courage and to love deeply.

When your skills and functions match your inner voice, you will discover peace and integrity. Very often you will also know true happiness. You will learn in this process the meaning of your life, and I hope, sense the integration of all the various pieces of your existence.

You are here ➡

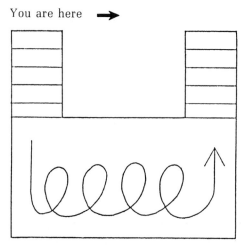

1: PRE-REQUISITE FOR THE JOURNEY

To journey inward and hear the voice of our hearts a certain skill is needed. As an ocean diver learns to swim before he explores the sea's floor, so we need to strengthen our powers of observation before we descend into the U process that leads to our whisper.

Becoming a *participant-observer* stands as the single pre-requisite to begin the U process. So important is this skill that I make it a goal everytime I begin psychotherapy with a client. No matter what goals the client has in coming to me, I always give him or her another. I say: "By the time this therapy is over, I hope you will be able to observe yourself, your thoughts and feelings, your behaviors and your personal interactions with others more thoroughly than you do now."

Observing our participation opens the door to the U process and serves as a hearing aid to the voice quietly speaking within.

Most of us participate in our lives. But few of us observe our participation. The father of a 16 year old boy was sharing his upset with himself for the way he responded to his son. The son usually came home past the 11 PM curfew time. The father wanted to know where the child went and what he did. The boy wouldn't tell him. The father would become enraged and verbally abuse his son. This same pattern had been going on for over a year. The father knew that his anger did not help the situation, but he continued acting in the same way.

Here was a man *participating* in his life, but not *observing* his participation. Consequently, he was not able to change the participation. If you want to change a feeling, reaction or behavior (your participation), then you help yourself by learning to *observe* well what is happening within you and outside of you.

The more you observe, the more information you will have about yourself. With information comes knowledge. (Recall Socrates', "Know Thyself.") When you have knowledge, you have options. With options you have choices to make. And when you make choices for growth, then you possess personal freedom. (Fig. 2)

Most people are able to do some observing of their participation; but the real skill lies in getting that observation to happen *while* the participation is going on. Many of us observe well *after* the fact. The father in the above example observed much later: "Darn, I did it again. I always get hooked by my son's silence." The effort here will be to move that observation closer and closer to the participation. Then change occurs more willingly.

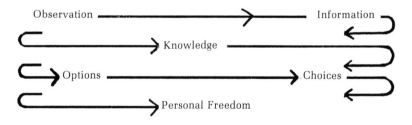

Originally, I had thought to call this book "Toilet-Training Your Mind" because the best explanation I know to describe the dynamics of a participant-observer can be found in the process of toilet training.

For approximately the first two years of life little Andy wet his diaper. He participated in urinating in his pants. But he did not observe his participation. Then, one day, well after he wet his pants, he became *aware* that the diaper was wet and he felt uncomfortable. His first observation had occurred, albeit well after his participation. But, now, the process of change was underway.

Time and again he participated in wetting. Afterwards he observed what was happening. Gradually, his observations occurred more closely to the wetting. One day, he wet and immediately afterwards he noticed his participation. He probably thought: "Oh my, I just did it. Look how soggy I am." Next time his observation occurred *while* he was wetting ("Oh, my God, I'm wetting right now"). At this point, he is almost ready for changing his participation in wetting. He notices the cues to wetting (a full bladder and discomfort). With this information, plus observations of his dad urinating in the toilet, little Andy now has options. He says to himself: "Either I can wet in my pants as I've always done, or I can do like Dad does." With those options, he has a choice to make. When he makes the choice to "do like Dad," he is free from a behavioral habit and wet pants. His observations led to freedom.

Understandably, when we are children, our ability to observe our participation is very limited. Observation is an adult skill. In Transactional Analysis, one of the adult functions is data-collection, the skill of observing how we operate. The child is a participator, simply reacting to his or her environment. The child in us learns significant beliefs about the self, and based on these beliefs acts accordingly.

Many of these beliefs feed into the child's self-esteem. Perhaps the child in you learned "If people respond negatively to something I say, it means they don't like me and I'm no good." So, when you are with people, you behave in a very shy manner in order to avoid making any mistakes that could cause a negative reaction in another. This is your way of participating in social settings.

Enter the adult. The observing adult in you begins to

notice that whenever you are with people you automatically take on a defensive stance because you are afraid of other people's negative reactions to you. You become aware of the childhood beliefs you have about yourself and others. You start to see how these beliefs make you dependent on others for your self-worth. You keep observing these beliefs and patterns of shyness and soon you realize you can think differently. You can take on new, more adult beliefs about yourself. You have a choice. You have control over your sense of self. Through observation you are led to *choose* to value yourself or not no matter how others respond to you. You have become free.

As you start to observe yourself more fully let me warn you of a pitfall. Observation generally leads to temporary pain and frustration. As you become more aware of yourself and your personal dynamics, you may feel discouraged because you might think: "Gee, look at all this mess. I have so far to go. I don't know if I can do it." Your frustration may increase when your awareness is sharp, your options lie before you and you still choose the old way of participating. Please, try not to get too down on yourself. Keep observing. Continue watching what you do and how you are operating inside. You can change. The adult can and will learn to direct the child in you.

The alternative is worse — a return to the slavery of your former patterns. If you participate without observing, you then find yourself trapped. Being trapped is perhaps the most uncomfortable and distasteful state any of us can experience. When people feel trapped in their way of participating in life, then they know unfreedom. And our human spirit despises unfreedom. "Born to be free," we yearn for choices. Sometimes we can feel so trapped and unfree that we create the ultimate option, suicide, in order to have a choice. Often, people who have considered suicide do not want to kill themselves as much as they want an alternative to a trapped position. Suicide, as an option, gives them the choice to say no to it.

Then, at least, they find a little freedom. So I encourage you to observe yourself, to "toilet-train your mind." As you do so, you will begin to notice signals at the top of the U. These signals turn us in the direction of our heart where the voice of truth speaks.

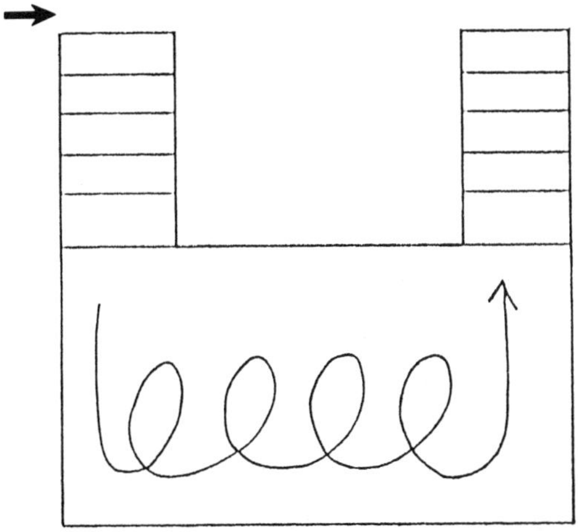

2: FEELINGS: SOUNDS OF THE HEART

Our emotions move within us as powerful sounds that echo the voice of our deepest self. Along with our behavior, our feelings circle around the top of the U, expressing directly or indirectly the movements of our inner core. To journey to our heart, then, we first observe and understand the language of feelings.

I once worked with a woman who could not identify her feelings. When she cried, I'd reflect "You seem very sad." She would respond: "I cannot find the answer." For her, feelings did not exist, only thoughts. She forever searched for answers. As a university professor, "answers" may have been easier for her to deal with than feelings. This was an impoverished woman. A major part of her life lay unknown to her.

No Morality to Feelings

Feelings are neither right nor wrong, good nor bad. They do not fall under the scope of moral principles. Anger is not awful. Oftentimes, it may not help us or others attain our goals. But, then, it is only unhelpful, not bad or evil. Depression is not wrong. We do not enjoy depressed moods, but we need not get guilty because we are depressed. That only fuels the depression.

In a group discussion one man acknowledged: "Five years ago I went to a therapist for depression. The most helpful thing she said occurred in the first session. She said it was OK for me to be depressed. I never knew that. It blew my mind. I thought somehow I was bad for being depressed. Getting depressed made me more depressed, if you know what I mean."

Another person in the group added: "I always find that after I'm depressed, I do some special growing. It almost seems like there's something good in depression."

Feelings can be helpful or unhelpful. They can lead you forward or push you backward. But try to get away from calling them good or bad, right or wrong. They are simply *there*. They are normal and common and ordinary. In fact, every feeling you experience comes from a perfectly understandable place in you. If you could know all that went before you, the way you processed life and the way you have seen the world, you would only say about your feelings: "Oh, that makes sense that I feel like this." You may not like your feelings; they may feel uncomfortable, but they exist. Period. No right or wrong about them.

At times you may hear yourself saying "I shouldn't feel angry. I shouldn't worry." Nonsense. You *do* feel angry. You *do* worry. No shoulds about it. Because the feelings exist they are *good* in one sense: they serve as signals of who you are down at the bottom of your U. Every feeling you own can tell you of your deeper self. So rather than shove "wrong and naughty" feelings aside because "good people shouldn't feel such things," I want to encourage you to learn your feelings by facing them and entering them. They can bring you to yourself.

How Your Feelings Work

We all have what Kurt Lewin, a social psychologist, once called a psychic map. This psychic map or personal domain reflects all the aspects of our life. Figure 3 shows what a personal domain might look like. Your domain is composed of all the people, events and things that have touched and entered your life. I, through this book, am now part of your domain. Certain elements occupy a large amount of your domain, while other parts take up very little space. Usually our significant relationships consume the greater part of our personal domain. (Figure 3)

Your emotions can best be understood as they relate to your personal domain. Generally, you respond with different feelings according to what happens in that domain. Three families of feelings result when your domain is affected:

1. depression - happiness
2. anxiety - calm
3. anger - peace

The psychologist, Aaron Beck, has identified these groups of feelings as a simple way to help us label our emotions.

Depression-Happiness

Depression-happiness makes up the first group of feelings. Depression is the sad feeling that occurs when you lose a significant and positive element of your domain. Whenever you find yourself depressed, look for a loss. Ask yourself: "What have I lost?"

Some losses appear obvious. Your best friend leaves town and a major part of your domain falls away. Your spouse or a child dies; you lose your job; your stock investments hits an all-time low; you get an F for your final grade; you do not get the promotion. All of these are obvious significant losses that generally bring on the sad mood we call depression.

Other losses may not appear so evident. You can lose the esteem of others and suffer serious depression. You can lose the esteem of yourself and experience a low-grade depression that seems to pervade your daily existence. You can lose a sense of meaning and purpose in life and feel lethargic and directionless. These losses are often covered over by perfectionism, over-compensation, "superiority complexes," aggressiveness, laziness and even anger. But try cutting through these defenses and ask yourself over and over: "What have I lost in my domain?" Knowing what you lost will help you know the cause of your depression.

Your losses can be real or imagined. Either way you will be depressed. If you see your wedding band being flushed down the toilet, your depression comes from a real loss. If you misplace the wedding band and cannot find it temporarily, the depression comes from an imagined loss. The next day you find it on the kitchen cabinet and the depression vanishes.

When you feel down because you believe you have lost the esteem of another person, that loss is often imagined. Most of us fear that others' judgments of us may be negative rather than positive. We make a public comment at a meeting and wonder how stupid we might have sounded. We then get sad because we incorrectly believe that everyone will be whispering about how dumb that guy was who made that silly comment. Our loss is imaginary, but nonetheless leads to depression.

When I give talks, I work hard to present a helpful message and to keep people awake. If someone falls asleep while I am speaking, I think he or she does not like what I am saying. I get sad thinking I have lost that person's esteem.

At times that loss is imagined. A man who had slept through much of the first half of my talk, came to me at the break, and said: "Pardon me for falling asleep during your talk. I'm a mailman and get up at 4:00 A.M. every morning. I go to bed at 8:00 P.M. It's already an hour and a half past my bed time." I stopped being sad about him sleeping because I realized I had not lost his esteem.

Losing or thinking we have lost the esteem of others plays havoc in us. I believe our focusing on other people's opinions of us is perhaps the leading cause of depression and stress. Much of this book involves an effort to de-focus our attentiveness on other's views, and to

Identification of Emotions

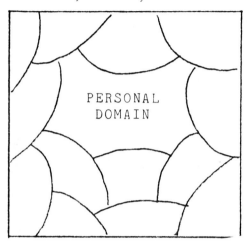

PERSONAL
DOMAIN

POSITIVE

Happiness
(An Intact Domain)
Excitement
Encouragement
Pride
Confidence

Calmness
(No threat to
the Domain)
Peace
Relaxation
Serenity

Contentment
(Sense that all laws
regarding the Domain
are being observed)
Tolerance
Acceptance

NEGATIVE

Depression
(Loss in the Domain)
Sadness
Hurt
Discouragement
Sense of worthlessness
Humiliation
Embarassment
Lack of confidence

Anxiety
(Impending danger
to an aspect of the Domain)
Worry
Fear
Tenseness
Nervousness

Anger
(Response to an outside
force that violates the laws
that protect the Domain)
Resentment
Frustration
Guilt
Jealousy
Envy

learn how to focus on the beauty and richness of our own inner energies. More on this later.

While the term depression sounds like a major sadness, there are other labels that suggest the same dynamic, namely the loss of a significant and positive part of your domain. *Self-pity* is a way of responding to loss. Feeling *down* or *blue* are forms of reacting to a loss in your domain. *Hurt* usually occurs when you experience some loss of love in a relationship. *Guilt* implies a loss of self-esteem. And *sadness*, of course, lays in you when the garden variety of daily losses occurs, such as rainy weather for a week.

Just a comment about anger and depression. Many people define depression as "anger turned inward." The definition holds considerable merit. Depression, in our society, seems much more socially acceptable than anger. Consequently, we often suppress and repress our angers, then convert them into depression. "I get angry with me" equals depression. That is, anger at myself causes a significant loss to my self-esteem. But loss still occurs. So even when anger is connected to your depression, still look for the loss. More about the connection between anger and depression-hurt in Chapter 6.

Briefly, the other side of depression is happiness. When you possess an intact domain, where nothing appears lost, then you have happiness. Also when you add to your domain, happiness results. The other day one of my staff members, a nurse, came into the office full of excitement. She had just given a talk to 200 nurses, who really appreciated it. Many of those nurses will probably make referrals to Mary at various times. She added that group to her domain. The result was happiness.

Anxiety-Calm

Anxiety occurs when you sense impending danger to your domain. When you think you are about to lose a significant piece of your domain, the emotion that rises up in you is fear. You step into an airplane for the first time (or the 50th time) and the knot you feel in your stomach tells you of your fear of losing your entire domain. Recently, my wife flew to North Carolina and *I* felt the anxiety — a fear of impending loss to my domain.

Some time ago we got a kitten for our children. She was prowling around outside and got into the neighbor's basement. They saw her come in their house, but could not find her. We all searched without success. She was nowhere. We went back home with some anxiety because our kitten had become a significant part of our domain. We worried over the possible loss. Our neighbors also experienced anxiety. All the while we were looking for the kitten, they kept asking: "Is she housebroken? Is she trained?" Their anxiety was the possible loss of a clean carpet. (In narrating this story to a friend, he suggested that anything the kitten might do during the night would actually *add* to my neighbor's domain!) By the way, the next day we found the kitten inside the neighbor's pool table. And no messes anywhere.

Which leads to the point...Most of the time, our anxiety is for naught. What we worried about does not, in fact, get lost. A couple of months ago, my wife, Joelyn, was scheduled to moderate a debate for candidates seeking school board positions. The debate was to be on cable TV in mid-April. For two weeks prior, Joelyn worried. The fear arose in this fashion: "I might not do well. If I don't I will look like a fool. Everybody in the whole world will see how dumb I am. I will lose their positive regard for me."

The morning of the debate — mid-April, remember — we received 10 inches of ice and snow. The debate was cancelled. Elections were the next day, so Joelyn never did moderate the debate. But she had worried about it for two whole weeks.

Now, you will not experience anxiety and depression over the same issue at the same time. For example, you receive a memo from your boss saying: "Please, come to my office at 3:30 PM today." Of course, you get the memo at 9:00 AM. All day you feel anxious, wondering what this is about. You know we are in a recession and employees have been laid off. Your anxiety rises as you sense the danger to your job — a significant loss to your domain. At 3:30 you enter the boss's office and he announces that you are to be laid off. Your anxiety immediately ceases, and depression begins. You are no longer in danger of losing; you have now lost a significant part of your domain.

Other parts of the anxiety family include fear, worry, panic and nervousness. Whatever the word you use, the dynamic remains the same — a sense of impending loss to the domain. When you feel yourself tied up in knots, stomach churning, muscles tense, head throbbing, butterflies floating, ask yourself: "What am I afraid of losing?" The answer will help you find the culprit that triggers your anxiety.

The more enjoyable side of anxiety is calm. When no dangers stand before your domain, when nothing threatens you, you experience relaxation and calm.

Anger-Contentment

The third family of feelings works to *protect* your domain. Anger signals a defensive response to a perceived attack against your domain. When no such attack is present, contentment and peace will fill you.

Here's how anger works. We set up rules around our personal domain as a wall to safeguard all that lies within. We make these rules easily and frequently. Within each of us sits a little legislator creating laws that others and we must live by. When these laws get broken, we respond with anger. I often make rules on how others ought to drive cars. When they break my rules, I get angry and call them jerks. My rules for drivers protect my domain from death, injury or at least inconvenience.

One of my rules for myself goes this way: "I must never be late for my therapy clients. I should always be on time." If I fall behind schedule, I become irritated with myself. This promptness rule protects me from los-

ing others' respect for me. I figure it like this: "Most of
the time physicians are late. Patients sit for long periods
of time, grumbling about the 'damn doctor.' I can avoid
people's grumblings about me if I am on time. They will
like me better than they like physicians!"

The rules we create to avoid losses are endless: "My
wife should support me; my friend should call me; the
sun should shine during my vacation; the kids should
come when I call; I should not be alone tonight; he
should not be angry with me," etc. Although we possess
vast legislative powers, unfortunately our executive
powers remain considerably limited. Thus, inherent
frustration results. And that frustration is part of the anger family. If you were elected to your state legislature
and began making laws, only to discover that the executive branch of government took a four year sabbatical,
you would experience a great frustration with your job.
This very dynamic happens within each of us, leading to
our frustrations and anger.

Let's return to the example of the boss calling you to
his office. You receive his message and become anxious,
fearing the possible loss of your job. You hear him tell
you at the end of the day you are laid off, and your
anxiety turns to depression because you have now lost a
significant part of your domain. On your way home you
start thinking about the other employees who did not get
laid off. You begin making some rules (after the fact, by
the way): "Joe should have been laid off before me. I
have seniority. The boss should have given me more
notice. The economy shouldn't be this rotten. The Re-
publicans should never have been elected." Your rules
have all been broken so you become angry.

Along with frustration, other elements in the anger
family include resentment, revenge, guilt and jealousy.
Resentment is a sustained disdain for someone who has
invaded your domain. Long after the event, we continue
imposing on that person the rule they once broke. I
believe resentment is one of the critical elements in the
breakdown of marriages. *Revenge* arises out of resent-

ment. It demands justice. One time I had to terminate a therapy relationship with a woman that had become clearly counterproductive. Understandably, she was angry with me. The anger continued and grew to resentment. Eventually, it became revenge, when for a period of time, she called me almost every early morning around 3:00 A.M. When I answered, she would hang up. She got back at me.

The feeling popularly called "guilt" usually occurs when we break rules for ourselves that are meant to protect our image before others. Most of the time "guilt" does not refer to "moral guilt." It is the "bad feeling" we have when we think we have done something that will gain disapproval from others.

Recently, a woman complained to me of her deep sense of guilt when she visited her mother-in-law in the nursing home. She claimed to be able to find no reason for the guilt feelings. I asked her if she ever wondered what the nursing staff thought of her. The light immediately went on. She said: "Oh, my God, I think all the time about them. I feel they think I'm a poor daughter-in-law, because we have a lot of money and I don't come to visit her except on Tuesdays." Her law was, "A good daughter-in-law visits her invalid mother-in-law daily, especially since she has the time. A good and wealthy daughter-in-law also brings expensive things every time she comes." The woman has these laws so that she can present a "perfect daughter-in-law" image to the nursing staff and, thus, not lose their positive judgment of her. The bad feeling she has when she losses their esteem she calls guilt.

Jealousy is part anger and part anxiety. We make rules about our friend's or spouse's behavior: "She should not talk friendly to other men." "He should pay more attention to me than to her." When our laws are broken by the other person, we react with a mixture of anger (we are trying to protect our domain) and anxiety (we sense impending danger to our domain.) In interpersonal relationships that mixture is jealousy.

In summary, remember this triple dynamic then: Depression is a signficant loss to our domain; anxiety is the sense of impending danger to the domain; and anger results from the breaking of the laws we make to protect our domain.

Happiness occurs when the domain is intact; calm follows the experience of no threats to the domain; and peace results when all our laws are being obeyed. These three families of feelings will be explored separately in Chapter 4, 5, and 6.

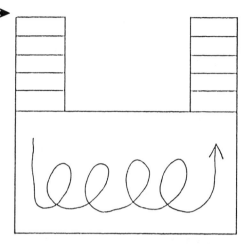

3: FIRST STEP TO THE HEART

As we begin the journey down the left side of the U, we first become *aware* of feelings. Our emotions open the door to our deepest spirit. But to reach that living center in us, we first need to recognize, enter and name our feelings.

When we encounter a feeling, we have two basic choices: either we can engage the feeling or we can avoid and deny it. The choice we make will generally be determined by our beliefs about emotions. If we engage our feelings, we probably believe:

It is good to feel things strongly.

Tears are often therapeutic.

Expressing anger keeps me free of stress.

Emotions are signs of something deeper in me.

I create my own emotions.

These kinds of beliefs lead us to appreciate our feelings and use them as stepping stones to our inner core.

But many people learned other beliefs, such as:

Emotions are dangerous things.

I shouldn't lose control of my emotions.

I shouldn't cry.

I shouldn't get angry.

I should be strong and tough.

If I know my feelings, I know myself.
Unpleasant feelings should be avoided at all costs.
I should immediately get rid of "bad" feelings.
I shouldn't show my feelings.
These beliefs lead us to deny or avoid our feelings.
Most of the above beliefs assume that uncomfortable feelings are bad and should be avoided. I think the majority of our powerful beliefs regarding feelings keep us away from them. Given these messages from our past, fleeing from our emotions seems quite understandable. Added to what we have learned, our nature's tendency is to avoid pain and discomfort and to seek pleasure and gratification. None of us, naturally, look for misery.

So, when unpleasant feelings rise up in us, we first attempt to separate ourselves from them. While I was in graduate school, a fellow student did some research on how young children deal with conflict. His results indicated the vast majority "flee the arena of conflict." They avoid it as fast as they can. What occurs in interpersonal conflict also takes place in intrapersonal disturbances — we tend to withdraw and avoid. We develop various strategies to accomplish this avoidance of our feelings.

Avoidance Strategies

The most obvious way to avoid something is to walk on the other side of the street. If I expect a nasty phone call, I simply keep the phone off the hook or stay away from home. If I don't want to get that big bill, I just stop opening my mail. If I don't like my in-laws, then I don't go visiting.

If I do not want uncomfortable feelings, I will not go inside myself. I stay operating in the external world. I can avoid my feelings by living my life at the outer edges of my skin. I have an acquaintance who can only talk about machines. He goes into great detail about how everything works, but I never know how *he* works. He stays away from feelings by living totally in the external world. Men, by the way, seem to use this strategy more frequently than women in our culture. We talk sports, cars, machines, money, business, but not too frequently about our feelings.

The alternative to externalizing things is to internalize them. Instead of avoiding feelings by living outside our bodies, we can *enter* our feelings. We can remember that our feelings are good signals that tell us something about ourselves. But even here, by going inside, we need to beware of a possible danger. When we enter our feelings we can do so in one of two ways:

1) We can engage the feeling in order to discover what lies under it, what life-giving energy stimulates it. We enter the feeling to learn who we are and how to live fully out of that awareness.

2) Or we can enter our feelings and become stuck in them. Depression lends itself well to this dynamic. By focusing too much on the depressive elements in life we can easily feed the depression. Let's say I get down because of rainy weather for the third day of my vacation. I enter myself attending to my depression, but not as a signal of something deeper in me, but only as an awareness of "lousy luck." I then can think "This *always* happens to me," thus generalizing my lousy luck to *all* my vacations. Then I can add a dose of self-pity and a bit of loneliness ("no one cares anyway"), and I have accelerated my down mood into a full scale depression. This kind of internalizing does not help.

Often when we internalize in this way we gain something for ourselves. When we hold onto unpleasant feelings for extended periods we usually get something back that we consider beneficial. Therapists often talk of this as the "payoff." I find clients do not like it when therapists say: "What's the payoff for holding onto your depression or anger?" Yet oftentimes, not always conscious to us, we believe it works to our advantage to hold onto an unpleasant feeling.

A woman told me of her deep resentment toward her husband. She emoted strongly and at great length about

how awful he treated her. She wanted to break the resentment, but said she could not. I asked her what would
happen if she gave up the resentment. After some
searching, it dawned on her: "If I stop resenting him, I
will have to give up my hope of ever being happy with
him." In other words, as long as she stayed angry with
him she could go on making rules on what he must
change, and hope one day he would respond to those
rules. To give up her resentment she would have to accept him as he was and understand that the way he had
acted was simply the way he had acted. She would have
to give up her belief that her rules would change him.
Without the resentment, she would have to conclude:
"He is the way he is. He might not change. And if he does
not change, our marriage is dead." So to avoid that terrible possibility she held onto her resentment.

Herein lies the neurotic trap. This woman used a
dynamic (her resentment) for a positive goal, namely to
keep her hope in the marriage alive. But as time went on
and her resentment grew, it began to yield very negative
effects on her. She was constantly irritable with her
children; she no longer enjoyed her home; she could see
nothing good in her husband; and he withdrew from her
the more resentment he sensed. Yet even though she saw
the destructive powers of her anger, she still could not let
it go because she sensed her marriage would then end.

We all have our little, and not so little, neurotic
binds. One of mine involves promptness, anxiety and
patience. When I fly, I must get to the airport in plenty of
time. Once I arrive and have checked my luggage and
gotten my seat assignment my anxiety is alleviated. That
works for me, and yields the payoff I need. But then I
have to *wait* and *wait*. I become impatient with waiting
for anything longer than one minute. Reducing my
anxiety by getting to the airport early results in impatience and being upset at having to sit around.

Specific Defenses Against Feelings

Keeping in mind that *observation* helps us enter our

emotions, I want to explain some of the main defenses people use to guard against unpleasant feelings. If any of these ring a bell for you, please try to notice when and where and how you use this defense. We will talk later about what to do. First, become aware.

Suppression stands at the head of our list of defenses. We all employ this one at times when we consciously stuff down feelings we have. Pleasant and unpleasant feelings alike succumb to suppression. My son learned at least by age six to suppress his expression of love for me. One day, while we were outside, he came over to me, looked around, saw no one was watching him, and kissed me, announcing: "I just kissed you in public, Dad." Somewhere, he already learned that boys do not show affection to their dads in public.

Examples of suppression abound: A wife asks her extra-quiet, scowling husband, "What's the matter?" and he replies "Nothing." A woman is irritated because her hamburger is cold, and when the waitress asks how everything is, she says "fine." A man puts off making an unpleasant phone call and gets busy with another project. A husband has a need to talk with his wife, but does not mention it. A friend needs a little space from another friend and does not ask for it. Anger, anxiety, intimacy, and tenderness are among the primary emotions that get suppressed.

One step deeper lies the defense of *repression.* This defense keeps the emotion out of our conscious reach. Closely related to repression is *denial.* In denial we insist that we do not possess any such feeling. Repression and denial keep us "out of touch" with ourselves.

In group therapy, one woman appeared very rigid and quite distant from the others. They encouraged her to participate more fully, but to no avail. They challenged her, confronted her, even cajoled her. She responded by announcing she was angry with the group, but said so without any inflection in the voice or any other cues to suggest anger. Five minutes later, when asked how she was feeling she said: "I feel calm and peaceful. I walked here today and the air was warm and the flowers were so pretty." She had been referred to the group by a therapist who told her she had "frozen anger." He certainly was right. It was so deeply repressed that she simply could not touch it when she first entered our group.

Anxiety also suffers much repression. Probably all of us have repressed our fear of death at one time or another. Only in the past couple of years have I acknowledged that someday I will die. I have been noticing how people my age suffer all kinds of fatal illnesses.

Deep-seated fears of openness, love, physical abuse, incurring negative judgments can all get repressed from early on in life. The fears sit within for years, but they do not sit passively. They build energy, and unconsciously we keep fighting the anxieties back. Imagine the energy drain on us! We fight feelings we are not even aware of. Eventually the fears "convert," that is, they take on different forms, and force their way out. They get expressed in tension headaches, backaches, in a myriad of physical complaints, in sudden panic reactions that do not seem to have a cause. All these responses can be repressed fears crying out for expression.

Projection protects us against our feelings by placing them outside of ourselves in some other person. We might say, with considerable irritation: "Jim always seems so irritable. I wonder what's the matter with him." We place our irritation onto Jim. In therapy, a man rejected me, but blamed me for rejecting him. In marriage, I often observe husband and wife projecting on each other. This is called the "mirror-image effect." We see in each other what exists in ourselves. The husband tells me, "She never has time for me." She says: "He never talks with me." They both perceive in the other what they vaguely dislike in themselves.

We can even project our feelings onto things. One man I knew experienced so much disorganization and anxiety within himself that he projected these feelings onto his car. He took most of his personal belongings, clothes, toiletries, tools, and organized them in his car. At any given minute he could find whatever he wanted because he labeled each item in the car. He organized his outside life as a response to his own inner deterioration that he could not face.

Another common defense is *intellectualizing*. Here, we *think* our feelings away. Very often the question "How do you feel?" gets a thinking response "I feel that the sun will never shine again." That is a thought, not a feeling. With intellectualizing we theorize about the realities of our lives rather than experience them.

One simple way you can check to see if you are intellectualizing is this: Watch your language. When you say "I feel..." see if the word "that" follows. If it does (as in "I feel *that* you are wrong"), then you presented a thought. It does not tell us how you *feel* about the other person being wrong. Feelings are expressed when you say, "I feel angry, happy, sad, frightened, calm, etc." The "I feel" needs to be followed immediately by a feeling word. "I feel *that*" is always a thought. Actually, thoughts are best expressed by "I *think* that," or "I *believe* that."

Many of us seem to have a natural tendency to live out of our heads. We analyze, want answers, seek solutions, but do not stay close to our feelings. Throughout this U process, I want to encourage you to *enter* your feelings. Certainly, you need to use your head in this process, but first you need to touch your feelings, learn to embrace them and discover what they have to tell you. Remember, they are signals not to be avoided, but engaged. Please let them have a chance to speak to you, no matter how unpleasant or powerful they might seem.

Later on we will investigate your thinking process, because your thoughts create your feelings. If you want to change feelings, you will need to work with your thinking. However, for now, try avoiding your head. And please do not ask yourself: "*Why* am I feeling like this?" The *why* question usually sends us into our heads on an endless journey in search of root causes. At this time, at

the top of the U process, only concern yourself with experiencing your feelings, knowing they are neither right
nor wrong. As signals they will tell you something of who
you are.
    Below is a list of words describing all kinds of feel-
ings. I would like to encourage you to go through the list
and identify the words that best express how you feel
and have felt in different situations. I also encourage you
to ask yourself, occasionally, throughout the day: "How
am I feeling right not?" and try to label it. After you name
the feeling, allow yourself a brief moment to intensify
that feeling in order to know it more fully.

Comfortable Feelings

Accepting	Energetic	Prosperous
Acceptable	Entranced	Patient
Admired	Euphoric	Proud
Adequate	Feminine	Poised
Amused	Friendly	Powerful
Amazed	Flabbergasted	Protective
Alive	Free	Perceptive
Affectionate	Fulfilled	Quiet
Animated	Fortunate	Rich
Appreciated	Fascinated	Romantic
Astonished	Gracious	Receptive
Beautiful	Generous	Refreshed
Bewitched	Glamorous	Respected
Bubbly	Gay	Revitalized
Buoyant	Giddy	Responsive
Calm	Grateful	Satisfied
Cared for	Gregarious	Seductive
Childlike	Happy	Sincere
Confident	Hospitable	Serene
Cheerful	Healthy	Safe
Considered	Hopeful	Sentimental
Contented	Impressed	Secure
Concerned	Important	Sociable
Composed	Intoxicated	Stimulated
Comfortable	Intelligent	Sensitive
Cordial	Inspired	Successful
Competent	Invigorated	Surprised
Capable	Interested	Spiritual

Cozy
Curious
Captivated
Creative
Delighted
Desirable
Deserving
Delirious
Expressive
Eager
Enthusiastic
Empathetic
Elated
Enriched
Effervescent
Excited
Ecstatic
Encouraged
Enjoyment
Enlightened
Enamoured
Enchanted

Included
Joyful
Jubilant
Lively
Lovely
Loved
Lucky
Looked up to
Masculine
Masterful
Needed
Overjoyed
Overpowered
Outgoing
Optimistic
Pensive
Purposeful
Peaceful
Productive
Passionate
Positive
Pleased

Sympathetic
Supported
Talented
Trusted
Thankful
Thoughtful
Trusting
Thrilled
Tranquil
Transported
Tenderness
Triumphant
Tactful
Uplifted
Understood
Understanding
Unemcumbered
Vivacious
Victorious
Vibrant
Virile
Worthy

Uncomfortable Feelings

Abandoned
Afraid
Agitated
Angry
Alone
At a loss
Annoyed
Apart
Appeased
Amazed
Bad
Bothered
Bored
Burdensome
Callous
Caged
Cold
Censored
Cornered
Confused
Controlled

Hostile
Horrified
Hateful
Held back
Hurt
Hysterical
Inferior
Immobilized
Impetuous
Immoral
Insecure
Imposed upon
Irritated
Inadequate
Indifferent
In the way
Ill at ease
Jealous
Left out
Let down
Lonely

Resentment
Restless
Resigned
Repelled
Repulsed
Repugnance
Sensitive
Scared
Shaken
Stubborn
Shocked
Stunned
Sad
Seething
Shaved
Susceptible
Stifled
Submissive
Subversive
Subdued
Tormented

Disinterested	Lukewarm	Tortured
Dejected	Melancholic	Threatened
Disappointed	Morose	Terrified
Discouraged	Manipulated	Tired
Depressed	Managed	Tolerated
Distressed	Maneuvered	Trapped
Defeated	Mixed up	Troubled
Disturbed	Mortified	Unhappy
Disgusted	Meddlesome	Unfeeling
Dull	Naughty	Uncared for
Dead	Negative	Unloved
Envious	Numb	Unreasonable
Embarrassed	Overworked	Uncomfortable
Endured	Out of control	Unwelcome
Emotional	Pessimistic	Unwanted
Exhausted	Passive	Unworthy
Failure	Placated	Used
Frantic	Picked on	Upset
Fidgety	Paralyzed	Undemonstrative
Fearful	Pain	Unconcerned
Frightened	Pressured	Unfaired against
Frustrated	Put-up with	Uneasy
Furious	Put down	Vulnerable
Fuming	Put-upon	Weak
Frantic	Pestered	Worried
Fussed	Perturbed	Weary
Grief	Rejected	Worthless
Guilt	Restrained	Wild

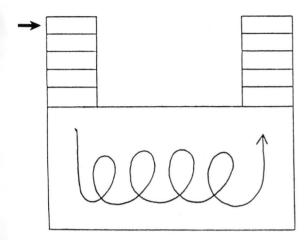

4: THE LANGUAGE OF DEPRESSION

In this and the following two chapters we will enter the three families of emotions more deeply. As you hear the sound of depression, anxiety and anger more keenly, you will begin to discern the whispers of your hearts. As you engage your feelings and understand their operations in you, you have a choice. Either you can continue to hold the pattern that keeps the feeling alive or you can opt to change the dynamic generating the feeling.

With depression, you will probably want to understand how it developed and how to *reduce* it. Where does it come from and how does it work? How do you feed it to keep it alive? How can you break depression's grip once it captures you?

Causes of depression vary. *External factors* can create depressive responses. If we really lose something significant and positive, we will become sad. We will enter a grieving process, part of which will include depression. First, we may deny the loss, not willing to believe that something or someone has been taken from our domain. Secondly, we may feel anger toward the cause of our loss. Thirdly, we flip to the depression as we focus on the loss to ourselves. Fourthly, we might try to negotiate a settlement, a way of covering our loss. And, finally, we usually come to accept the loss.

This kind of depression we have all experienced. None of us escapes significant losses in our lifetime. So we all experience this form of depression. Any significant loss, from our cat straying away from home for a week, to a close friend or relative dying, will trigger depressive feelings. When I decided to marry, part of that choice involved the realization that Joelyn or I would eventually die. That loss would be so painful for us. I wondered if it was worth it. Of course, I became aware that the normal journey through life would be filled with meetings, friendships, relationships and endings. I could not avoid the inevitable pain of loss in the loving relationships that have and would occur.

Externally induced depressions do not reflect any kind of psychological pathology. Reactions of intense sadness and grief over loss are normal and to be expected. If the sadness remains at a high level and significantly interferes with your life after an extended period of time (six months to one year), then you are probably feeding the depression by your thoughts and beliefs. At this point, you need to take more control over your inner functioning. I will show you how in a few minutes.

A second cause of depression come from within us. Internally induced depression causes more difficulty because we may not be able to identify its source. This tends to appear as a more stable, less dramatic form of sadness. Therapists often refer to it as "low-grade depression." It creates a pall of lethargy, tiredness, pessimism, crabbiness and negativity that affects everything we do.

This depressive state grows up out of long-standing beliefs, many of which were formed in childhood. These beliefs about ourselves, others and the world around us, generate depressive feelings. Examples of such beliefs include: "I can't do anything right." "No one ever loved me." "Other people are better than me." "Everything I touch turns sour."

With such beliefs coloring our every perception, we can easily see how our depression is caused from within us.

Finally, a third cause of depression is genetic, chemical and/or biological dysfunctioning. More and more evidence appears to suggest that some types of depression are related to changes in our physical make-up and functioning. Oftentimes, depression caused from these factors is best treated by medication.

At the present time, the *type* of depression a person experiences is best determined through a psychological interview. Consequently, very few "for certains" exist in determining the type of depression. Yet, we can get a pretty good sense based on any history of depression in the family, any circumstances of loss in one's present life, and the kind of thought patterns that accompany the depression.

Now, I want to focus on internally created depressions, because we have considerable power over these. We cannot do much about real losses in our lives, but learn to accept them. And with biologically related depression, we need to turn to medication. But we can learn to modify the depressions that arise out of our belief and thought structures. And, here, even externally induced and biologically related depressions may be aggravated by our beliefs and thought patterns.

The first step in reducing depression is to believe that *you* create it. Certainly, you need the triggering event, but more important, your thoughts and beliefs *about* the event generate depression. If your way of thinking about an event creates your emotion, then you can recognize your power to change the emotion by changing the thoughts. With the realization that you create your own emotions comes the awareness that you have the power to change your feelings. You are not enslaved by them, but you are in charge of your feelings.

Particular beliefs kick up depression. These beliefs stand as our real enemies. To free ourselves from the depressive feelings, we are helped to identify these beliefs in us, and then challenge and counter their accuracy. Just because we believe something to be true does not make it true.

Depressive Belief One

The first set of beliefs leading to depression has to do with *selective attention to negative experiences.* If I look out my window today and only see dead autumn leaves, and not the clear, crisp, sunny fall sky, I may depress myself, thinking "Oh, winter is coming in a month. What lousy weather. Nothing ever goes well. We always have awful weather in Wisconsin."

Depression can be caused by a narrowed vision of reality, a vision that picks up only the negative aspects. By focusing on the negative, we give it power. It gradually becomes the *whole* reality. Herein lies a fundamental principle in managing depression: *We give power to what we focus on.* When we attend to some negative event, we gradually make if bigger in our perception, and block out more and more the positive events. Eventually, all we see is the terribly depressing moments of life.

Recently, a man with depression shared his view: "Whenever my wife and I go to a party, she is happy, talkative and delightful. But at home she isn't like that. She doesn't talk much, seems serious and doesn't have fun. I doubt that she loves me anymore. I think she would rather be with other people than me."

Those conclusions ("I doubt that she loves me," etc.) arise from a narrowed view focused on negative aspects of reality. And those conclusions lead to depression. What this husband failed to see was all the other caring responses from his wife. He missed hearing her ask: "How are you feeling today?" or saying "Darling, I love you." He cannot see or remember the little gift she bought him last month for no apparent reason at all. And so on.

Sometimes when people perceive the negative to the exclusion of the positive, I ask them to keep a daily diary record of all the events they enter and to evaluate them as positive, negative or neutral for themselves. Consistently, these "negative thinkers" experience more positive than negative or neutral events. They simply do not focus on them.

Sometimes depressed persons selectively attend not only to negative events, but to *irrelevant factors*. Then, they apply negative meaning to the insignificant elements. Let's say I notice my wife gave larger scoops of ice cream to the kids than to me (irrelevant event). But I apply this meaning: "See, she favors them over me. I'm nothing to her." And I become depressed. Once again, I focus only on a small piece of reality. A key to life without depression is to keep seeing the *whole* picture, not just a part of it.

So, to break free from this negative thought pattern, keep challenging yourself to attend to *all of reality*, not just the negative. Acknowledge the negative, do not deny its existence. But, after recognizing it, notice also the positive elements and give yourself over to them.

Depressive Belief Two

"I can't do anything right." "Everything I touch flops." "I am a real loser," are some the of the ways this belief gets expressed. People who depress themselves often use the *high standard of excellence* beliefs. Internally, they set extremely high standards for themselves, and then believe that anything short of attaining that goal is failure.

They perceive only two alternatives: complete success or failure. No *degrees* of achievement exist. A father of six children complained to me of depression. In exploring his beliefs the cause was clear: He believed he must be "the best father in the world." Why? Because he was "put on this earth to advance the welfare of the world and the way to do that was by raising the finest children the world could know." When he became angry with them for doing kid things, he then concluded: "I am a failure as a father. Good fathers wouldn't yell at their kids and get upset."

The problem here lies in the dramatic jump from "best father in the world" to failure. Are there not degrees of good fathering? This dramatic leap causes considerable depression. The 15-year-old girl who breaks out with an acne attack attempts suicide because she believes her prettiness has been destroyed. Now she is "ugly." Either she must have a perfectly clear complexion or kill herself. A wife does not feel like having sex some night and so jumps to the conclusion: "I must be an awful wife." Either be sexy all the time or conclude you are sexually frigid and a lousy marriage partner.

Once again, you can see how the first depressive belief (thinking negatively) also enters here. These people only focus on the non-attainment of the full goal. Without reaching that, there is failure. They are blinded to all the degrees of success in between.

Depressive Belief Three

People depress themselves by believing that *their successes are externally caused and their failures are internally caused.* When "things go right" it is due to other people's efforts, good luck, a good hammer or a full moon. When "things go wrong" it is "my fault."

The hostess makes delicious cream puffs for dessert. When I compliment her she replies: "Oh, it was nothing. The recipe is so simple and I have an excellent oven." I turn and say to the husband: "Your lawn is just beautiful this year." He says: "We've had so much rain, that's why."

But if the cream puffs flop, the wife says: "You know, I just can't cook. I must not have followed the directions accurately." And when fungus appears in the man's lawn, he comments: "I should have stayed on top of that lawn. Sometimes, I just let things slide."

Many of these beliefs that assign fault to ourselves for failures and credit to others for successes probably arise from our training in humility and pride. The humble person gave credit to God and others for his/her achievements. Parents did not want their children to "get big heads" so downplayed their accomplishments. But when the "C" appeared on the report card, then it was the child's fault. "You don't concentrate enough at school."

So children turn into adults developing a pattern of thoughts that blinds them from recognizing their powers to achieve, and keeps them focused, instead, on failure. With that orientation, many people make the next step easily: They learn to believe they, themselves, are failures. And we have depression.

Depressive Belief Four

Close on the heels of the above belief regarding success and failure comes its companion attitude, namely, *learned helplessness.* If I am never the cause of good things, then I learn to believe I have no power to correct the negative. I begin to see myself as a victim without control in my own life.

Certainly, situations exist that we cannot control. But the helpless person believes he/she is trapped with no way out. The emotional response to helplessness is depression, lethargy, and loss of energy. Victims give up.

Most victims believe further that they do not have any power even over their feelings. This leads to more depression because they cannot get free from their depression. And that is depressing. In other words, the sense of helplessness feeds and intensifies the depression.

Depressive Belief Five

People who get depressed tend to orient toward *immediate gratification rather than delayed gratification.* This orientation also accelerates depression that already exists. Mothers at home with their children often move toward immediate gratification. By 4:00 P.M., Mom has had it. She needs a reward right now. So, she opens the refrigerator and consumes the rest of the chocolate cream pie. Afterward, she get depressed for eating because she is trying to lose weight. Delayed gratification would work like this: Mom has had it at 4:00 P.M., wants to eat, but says no. Instead, she decides to wait until the end of the week and then get that sweater she has been eyeing the last two weeks.

Since people tend to lose energy during depression, they often give in to the urge to do nothing. The alarm goes off, and they stay in bed. Or they get up only to sit at the window staring out for hours at a time. They are gratifying themselves for the moment, giving in to the lethargy they feel. But they become more depressed because they keep putting their jobs in jeopardy and cease attending to family, home and friends.

Depressive, immediate gratification shows up in two other ways. The first is *procrastination*. When we have something to do that we do not enjoy, we may gratify ourselves immediately by not doing it. That feels momentarily good. But the item hangs over our head, gnawing away at our conscience. That can lead to or feed a depression. Our jobs pile up — the phone calls we should make, the term paper that is due, the windows that need washing. We think, "It's all too much; I'll never get out from under these tasks I must do."

The other form of immediate gratification is *withdrawal*. If we are in conflict with someone, avoidance may be our strategy of dealing with the problem. Somehow we possess a magical belief that by avoiding a problem it might just go away. If you recall, when we were children and the teacher asked for an answer we did not know, we put our heads down and often closed our eyes so she would not call on us. I guess we believed if we could not see her, then she could not see us. But she still called on us.

As adults, we still often employ that old childhood

belief and try avoiding the conflicts and problems of our daily lives. We do not talk about our feelings with our marriage partner, our employer or our friend. We do not engage the difficulties in relationships, and so let them eat away at us. Not facing the issue or person is immediately gratifying; but ten minutes or three weeks later the problem will most likely still exist. We have carried it within us, which can be quite depressing.

Getting Free From Depression

We help ourselves most in overcoming depression by realizing that we have considerable power over it. Much of the depression we create by our beliefs and thoughts. So if we create it, we can also undo it in the following ways:

1. Focus on positive, life-giving aspects of reality.
Remember the principle I stated earlier: We give power to what we focus on. If we continually attend to the negative aspects of an event, we will stay depressed. We have some power to focus away from the negative. And we can increase that power through hard work and practice.

Choosing what to focus on and sticking with it is a form of discipline. I think of it as jogging in our minds. In our society, we have become quite capable of physical discipline and exercise. We take much better care of our bodies than we did 20 years ago. It has demanded considerable discipline and hard work to get the proper exercise and eat the right foods. What we have done physically, we can also do psychologically.

We can do ourselves a great favor by entering the tough discipline of psychological focusing. Try to think of yourself as addicted to a particular way of thinking and viewing the world. This negative depressive view leads to your sadness. You want to break the addictive pattern. So you need to work at it like any alcohol or drug-addicted person would work. You *force* yourself to stay away from the negative thoughts, and you do it for one *day* or *one hour* at a time.

As soon as your mind flips to the negative view, you jump on it, force yourself to attend to any positive aspects you can discover. Certainly, you will not feel better spontaneously. Quick cures generally do not last. You are trying to change a whole pattern of thinking. Here is where discipline comes to play. Jogging once around the track does not help at all. Passing up dessert one evening will not put us in shape. You are trying to teach yourself new patterns of behaving that will be helpful to your body. So do not expect instant relief of depression once you force yourself to new *patterns* of viewing and believing. That takes time since you are fighting old patterns that you have been practicing for 20 to 60 years.

A word of caution: By advising you to focus on the positive, I am not saying to *deny* the negative. No. I want you to live in the real world. The real world does hold negative aspects. I want to encourage you to recognize both the negative and the positive. Acknowledge them, and then choose to focus on the positive. Work with life, not death. Maybe that is the meaning of that troublesome scripture passage where Jesus said: "Let the dead bury their own dead."

2. Become aware of your depressive beliefs and challenge them.

Most of us become aware of our depressive *feelings*, but not so aware of our thoughts that create them. Explore your *thoughts*. What are you thinking when you get down? What old beliefs sit deeply in you that might trigger this depression? The beliefs I discussed earlier are among the most popular for depression.

Once you know what beliefs trigger the depression, you can begin challenging them. Just because you believe certain things does not make them true. You will help yourself by being willing to challenge any beliefs you have come to hold as true, especially if those beliefs lead to sadness and depression.

Challenging your beliefs and countering them with

new beliefs is the subject of many popular books and articles these days. Ways of challenging thoughts were probably first popularized by Albert Ellis, Ph.D., in a book called *A New Guide to Rational Living.* The principle in all these writings, and one I adhere to is this: Our beliefs and thoughts create our depressive feelings. By changing our beliefs and thoughts we gradually also change the depressive feelings.

3. When depressed, make yourself do physical things.
More often than not, depression tends to "de-energize" us. We do not feel like doing anything. We want only to sit and stare, or lie and sleep. We simply cannot get the energy to do anything. We have little motivation for action.

Of course, a major problem looms with inactivity. It allows our minds to zero in on the depressive element. Furthermore, we begin to feel even worse because we are doing nothing. "How worthless can I be?" is the thought that then arises.

To break the vicious circle of depression it is vital for people to stay physically active. If that means forcing yourself out of a chair to walk to the drug store, then do it. You do not have to jog five miles or "pump iron." But you do need to move.

Recently, I encouraged a depressed woman to climb up and down her basement stairs five times a day. Anything that gets you moving again is valuable when you are losing energy, motivation, and interest due to depression.

4. Set realistic short-term goals
We usually feel good when we accomplish a goal. When we are depressed, any positive feeling we can create will aid us. Often times, we set large, non-specific goals that become unreachable even if we were not depressed.

January first stands as *the* day for setting long-term goals. "I will love my wife more;" "I will be patient with the kids;" "I will not talk about people behind their backs." January second, we break them all, get discouraged (a form of depression), and revert to our old patterns.

Part of our depression will often revolve around failing to reach our ideals and goals. So set lesser goals, more simple attainable goals. There is nothing sacred about all the ideals we have had driven into us. I would rather see people accept lovingly their reality and letting go of some of their ideals, than holding desperately to their ideals and invalidating their realities.

Simple goals during depression might be: "I will spend at least one minute talking with and showing interest in my son when he comes home from school today." "I will read at least 20 pages from that text book I've been avoiding." Make it simple, realistic, and clear. Then do it. Success helps us feel like we are *gaining* something rather than *losing* something. And gaining feels like the opposite of depression.

5. Form your identity on being rather than function.

Perhaps the most serious cause of depression lies in the cultural belief that what you *do* makes you good or bad. We have become so preoccupied with how we function that we live continually in a precarious and dependent position. If we are good and valuable only when successful, then we are all doomed to periods of time (for some, extended periods of time) when we will feel bad and useless. Then we will depress ourselves because we will de-value who we are.

To truly become free from much depression, we need to learn to form our identity on our *being*, not our *doing*. If I know who I am at my center and I accept that, then successes and failures in my functioning will only be that — successes and failures. but they will not touch my worth, my "okayness," because *being* is not dependent on *doing*.

I will discuss this more fully in Chapters 7 through 11. I am convinced that if people get a feel for this distinction and could learn to live more fully out of their being, depression would become like measles after immunization.

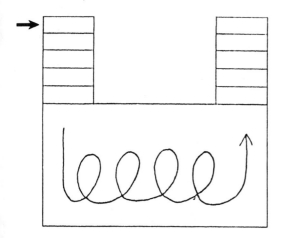

5: THE LANGUAGE OF ANXIETY

As depression can be used as a signal of the heart, so also can anxiety. This emotion speaks a language common to all of us. But its very familiarity sometimes makes it difficult to understand. And if we fail to understand anxiety, we will likely miss the whispering voice speaking within.

Historically, psychologists and psychotherapists have viewed anxiety as the basis of neurosis. Under all the manifestations of emotional and psychological dysfunctioning lies this gnawing villain. The longer I do psychotherapy, the more I come to believe the truth of this premise. Time and again, I discover deep-seated anxiety moving within the depths of persons troubled by neurotic complaints.

Anxiety can best be understood as the feeling we have when our very existence is threatened. Certainly, the threat can be to our physical life, as when we enter the hospital for major surgery. We may lose our life. So anxiety arises in us. But further, we can experience threats to our psychological life as well. Anxiety will rise up in us if our sense of meaning in life is threatened. We will feel anxious with the loss of self-esteem. Anxiety, then, always has to do with our physical or psychological existence. When death, in its many forms, faces us, we will experience anxiety.

Fear differs from anxiety. Fear is the response to specific threats to portions of our domain and is attached to definable objects that create the fear. The popular phobias regarding snakes, heights, new situations, enclosed spaces, etc., are called fears because they relate to specific objects. Fears do not directly touch the core of our being.

Fears seem to operate at the outer edges of our life; while anxiety springs from our deeper, inner self. In part, fears can help keep us away from our anxiety. One agoraphobic woman (afraid to leave home) had a fear of losing control of her surroundings. Thus, she stayed home. As her therapist worked with her, they uncovered a deeper anxiety of her own death and that of her mother. Oftentimes, when the deeper anxiety is revealed, the fear disappears. Of course, the anxiety causes considerable discomfort, but at least it can be worked with since it is out in the open.

Rollo May compared fears to the little battles that go on out in the fields. As long as a nation can keep the battles out there (fears), it can protect the capital city. But if the fear is destroyed or taken away, the inner citadel may be threatened.

So, anxiety is our response to the possible loss of our existence. Often, anxiety is normal. It should be there. It works for us. But just as often, it works against us. It becomes neurotic. In his book, The Meaning of Anxiety, Rollo May points our four elements to normal anxiety.

First of all, it is proportionate to the objective threat. If you hear your back door opening in the middle of the night, and everyone you know who should be inside is, then you will experience anxiety. It is normal if your heart begins to race, you wake up your partner, and then quickly call the police. It is neurotic, if you are so panic-struck that you cannot move. You lay there in a frozen trance.

The second element in normal anxiety is non-repression. In neurotic anxiety, the feelings get repressed so that the individual loses awareness of it. Repressed anxiety usually raises its head sooner or later either directly in anxiety attacks or indirectly in psychosomatic problems or in some other neurotic behavior. In normal anxiety, the person acknowledges his/her anxiety. Aware of it, the individual can say "I am scared to death."

The third element in normal anxiety is the absence of any other neurotic defenses against it, such as denial, projection, over-compensation, etc. If the robber breaks into the house, and we crawl deeper under the covers, saying "I didn't hear anything," then our anxiety is neurotic. Many people use denial with physical ailments. They do not go to the doctor with the persistent pain. They ignore bodily signs that something is wrong.

Compensation is a common defense against anxiety. Workaholics have to keep going, perhaps to cover a deep anxiety that might appear if the individual stopped for a moment and became quiet.

In normal anxiety, the fourth element is the anxiety can be confronted directly and constructively. In other words, we experience anxiety; we are aware of it; we acknowledge its presence; and we respond to it and the situation in realistic and appropriate ways.

Causes of Anxiety

As I suggested earlier, anxiety arises when we experience a threat to our physical or psychological existence. Death, then is cause for anxiety. But death comes in a variety of forms, other than physical destruction.

Perhaps the most significant threat to us other than physical annihilation is separation. Most of us want to feel connected to others. When we feel bonded to others we experience security, which I believe is the opposite of anxiety. But, when we sense that no one is there for us, that we are alone in the world, then anxiety begins to grow in us.

As a therapist, I have always been oriented toward people's present difficulties. I am not a historically oriented therapist. However, when someone comes to me with fears or vague anxieties, I then want to explore the history of their interpersonal relationships. Inevitably, we discover patterns of insecurity and aloneness, usually from infancy onward. Separation and isolation then become a critical issue in the problem of anxiety.

Deep within our human nature, I believe, lies an energy for social bonding. When we achieve such connectedness, we feel fulfilled and safe. We say things like "As long as I have you, nothing can be too hard to bear." We feel right and strong in our relationships with others.

When we relate well to others we experience our existence in a full way. Gabriel Marcel, the Christian Existentialist, linked relationships to the proof of our existence. He remembered the philosopher, DesCartes' dictum "I think, therefore I am," and disagreed saying "We are, therefore I am." Marcel believed that we know our own existence in relationship to others. In effect "I know I am here because you are there responding to me."

Now, in childhood, relationships play a central role in reducing anxiety. If the child feels accepted by the parents and loved dearly, independently of how he or she performs, that child will probably grow up relatively free from any neurotic anxiety. On the other hand, if the child experiences systematic rejection or conditional loving from the parents, the chances of neurotic anxiety increase significantly.

The classic picture of anxiety through separation occurs between infant and mother. If the relationship between mother and child is threatened in any way, anxiety can occur for the child. For example, let's say the child breaks a special dish. Mom becomes furious and yells: "Get out of here, you clumsy ox. I never want to see you again." If these messages occur with some frequency, the child will learn that he or she is lovable only if his or her performance satisfies mother.

Consciously the young child cannot deal with

mother's disapproval. He/she is helpless in the face of that threat. So the child represses the whole experience, but continues to fi ᵑht off the anxiety by pleasing mother. However, the child will never be quite sure if what he or she does really will win Mom's approval.

The child grows up, then, having developed a pattern whereby he or she desperately looks for approval from others, by performing as perfectly as possible. By acting perfectly the child-adult keeps the anxiety of separation and disapproval out of consciousness. However, while that perfectionist strategy works for a while, the individual is still never quite sure his/her behavior is perfect enough; nor is the person ever sure that no matter how perfect the behavior is, other people will accept it or the the person doing it. Thus, sadly, the person lives in a continued state of ambiguity and of inner pressure to keep performing at some peak level that will assure the approval of others.

Another cause of anxiety, then, lies in our drive to be successful. Perhaps one of the highest values in our culture is achievement and success. If we are successful, then we have value and assign worth to ourselves. We tend to form our identity on how well we achieve. If we are not successful, then we are nothing. In effect, we do not exist except through achievement. And there it is again, the threat to existence. Anxiety arises.

Our anxiety becomes intensified by the spirit of competition present in the success-oriented atmosphere. Generally, success means being the best in the field. Standing out as best implies others struggling to assume my position. I develop the mind set of a ladder, with me on a higher or lower rung. I do not always have control over which rung I stand on. Not having control over my success status means not controlling my sense of personal worth, since worth is tied to success. So I do not control my own sense of value. That creates significant anxiety.

Closely related to death, separation, and worth as causes of anxiety is *meaning* in life. If I do not have a

sense of meaning and purpose in life then I easily begin
to wonder: "Why bother existing?"

Our sense of meaning rests on three pillar. If you
pictured meaning as a building it would be supported by
three substructures.

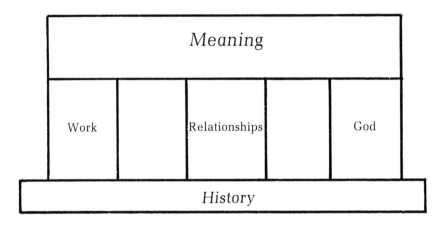

They are *work, relationships,* and *God* or some
transcendent being or purpose. If these three pillars
stand firm and well-balanced, anxiety will probably not
invade us. Unfortunately, for many of us, these three pillars tend not to be of equal strength. We often develop
one pillar to the detriment of the others.

Many men in our culture so focus on the work pillar
that their relational life and God pillar become weak.
Their meaning lies in their work. But look what happens
when the economy turns bad. They may lose their jobs,
and then what? Anxiety springs up, not only because
they do not know where to find the next job, but also because their sense of purpose in life was tied so exclusive-
ly to that one pillar. As it comes crumbling down, the
other two pillars cannot hold up the sense of meaning.
These men's very existence is threatened (anxiety). The
loss of meaning then gives way to depression.

Often in our culture, women have put much energy
into the relationship pillar, especially relations with
family and children. When the kids have grown up and

left home, women have felt great anxiety, because their sense of purpose was ended.

Spiritually oriented persons who put too strong an emphasis on their God pillar also feel great anxiety when they experience the "dark night of the soul."

Consequently, too much emphasis on any single pillar of meaning will most likely lead, at some point, to anxiety and loss of purpose. Clearly, the antidote is to develop all three pillars, so when one is weakened, we can shift to the others. At times when all three pillars are down, we turn to our histories to *remember* when we were important and had meaning. (A comment about this: Elderly people tell stories of their past to give continued meaning to their lives. Perhaps their friends and loved ones have died, their work is ended and God seems distant. To offset this void in meaning, they remember their past. One wonderful gift we can give them is to listen to and receive their stories. It helps them have meaning now by remembering when they once felt important and useful.)

The presence of sustained, on-going anxiety generally signals some basic inner conflict. Inevitably, the poles of the conflict are independence VS dependence, or the individual VS the community. The struggle within is an attempt to gain balance between being alone or with others, being intimate or distant. Often, a person wants intimacy, but fears it; or a person wants space and some aloneness, but fears it. So the individual vacilates in a state of tense ambiguity.

The probability of experiencing this inner conflict is high for all of us, because built into our nature are two powerful energies toward freedom and love. These two energies fit well together in the person living an interdependent life. However, the energies of freedom and love can set up the basis for considerable inner conflict. Freedom moves us toward independence, love toward a form of dependence.

We see this conflict present in young children, who one moment seem so mature and independent, and the next moment are very dependent. This vacillation is symbolic of the turmoil present in the neurotically anxious adult.

Working With Anxiety

The effort in dealing with anxiety is to attain a balance between aloneness and togetherness. In order to achieve such a balance, we need a basic sense of ourselves and an acceptance of who we are. (The second section of this book will explore how this acceptance can be accomplished.) This is particularly difficult for people who have not experienced unconditional love from their parents. It is these people who will most likely experience on-going anxiety.

Not enough can be said about that early childhood relation to mother and father. If the child does not experience the parents' deep abiding love, he or she will not know "basic trust." The child will not rest secure in the affection of the parents; but instead will forever wonder if he or she is lovable.

I have come to believe that if the child has not experienced basic trust with the parents, it leaves a certain void in his/her life that does not get filled in easily, if ever. The voided child will react in a number of possible ways. He or she will hungrily search out loving relationships anywhere. This person's appetite for love is unquenchable. The love of his/her partner or friend is never quite enough. On the other hand, the person might back away from all relationships, claiming not to need anyone. Another popular strategy for filling in the void is to win love and affirmation by "doing good things" for others.

All of these strategies never quite accomplish the goal of filling in the void. So the deeper anxiety remains, namely the fear "I do not count for anyone."

To work realistically with this anxiety springing from a childhood void, a couple of steps can be taken: First, the person is helped to explore with someone the childhood relationships with the parents. As you do that, allow yourself all the feelings that surface. Remember, feelings have no morality. They simply exist. This exploration allows you to resurface all that has been buried. That in itself is helpful. Furthermore, you might well become aware that much of your present behavior arises from your beliefs as a child. In other words, the old child in you still dictates how you are to operate now. Once you know that, you can choose to continue functioning out of the child, or you can choose to respond out of an adult stance which would counter those old childhood beliefs.

Secondly, it is helpful to assume that the voided place in your heart will never be filled again in life. Although difficult to hear, accepting this fact leads to considerable relief. No longer do you have to desperately search to be filled up by someone's love.

However, by accepting the voided spot in your heart, you need not give up all hope for happiness. You can certainly live a satisfying and fulfilling life, even with this "psychological handicap" or limitation. People with physical handicaps generally manage very well. We can do the same with our psychological limitations. We need not be psychologically perfect in order to attain happiness.

Once you accept the void, then you have two moves to make. First, you need to make an act of faith in your inner goodness. This is an adult act. By an act of faith, I mean a conscious, deliberate choice to believe that you are loveable and good independently of your life's experience. The act of faith may not *feel* convincing; but that is what makes it an act of faith and not an act of feeling.

It is practical to make an act of faith in your own goodness. We make acts of faith in all sorts of realities because our faith helps us. We do not always *feel* positive about life after death, but we choose to believe there is life after death because it alleviates fear and anxiety and satisfies our drive to exist. We make acts of faith every time we cross a bridge or stand on the 43rd floor of a sky-scraper, or at the top of the St. Louis Arch. We may not *feel* comfortable, but we still believe the structure will remain standing.

So, too, with ourselves. It works to our benefit to believe in our own goodness and worth. (Again, in the next section of this book, I hope to give you strong evidence to reinforce your act of faith in yourself.)

The second move you need to make is to go toward people in a self-revealing and understanding way, without demanding a lot in return. When you reveal yourself to someone without masking in any way, you will be liked. If you think of people you like and do not like, it has to do with masking. We tend to like people who share their inner lives with us, who do not fake it. We do not like people who play roles, e.g. know-it-alls, authorities, comedians. So if you want to feel loved and connected, then it helps to be self-revealing.

Furthermore, if you listen well and understand another person, you and they will feel a bonding. You have stood with them in their experience. Together, you will no longer feel alone.

Overall, the formation of loving community stands as the basis for overcoming the isolation and anxiety we know. Structures such as marriage, family, religious life, and church are intended to serve this purpose. Sometimes they do and sometimes they do not. I believe the struggle toward wholeness and life without neurotic anxiety lies in our ability to form community wherever we can. Certainly, we will reach differing levels with various persons and groups. But the movement toward bondedness with others, arising out of a freedom that comes from a true love of self, will help us deal most effectively with the deep anxiety inherent in human life.

Associated with an appropriate love of self in reducing anxiety is our ability to focus on *being* rather than *doing* for our worth and value. To resolve one of the fundamental causes of anxiety, namely the need to be successful in order to be worthwhile, we desperately need to learn to shift from our attentiveness to doing to a concern for being. This counter-cultural process takes considerable work, because we have been raised to believe we are what we do. The processes whereby we can make the shift from doing to being are presented in Chapter 7 through 11. For now, suffice it to say, our value is in who we are, not in what we do.

Ultimately, the preceding statement only makes sense when we have some kind of cosmic or religious view that frames our being. Throughout the ages, people and cultures have created ways of representing God, the reason for creation, life after death and so on. All of these representations have, in some way, served the useful purpose of reducing anxiety. (Certain views have also intensified anxiety!) They most effectively reduce anxiety when they view human beings as the result of the creative action of God or conscious cosmic force.

When a human artist creates a picture or a statue, he or she only wants it to *be* what it is. The creator does not ask it to *do* much, but only to *be* itself. If we, as persons, are the result of some creative action of a conscious God, then perhaps this God only wishes us to *be* as fully human as we can. Certainly, that means *doing*, but it does not demand total success. Certainly, there is no demand for reaching the top of the ladders created by the society in which we live.

But what is the purpose of *being* as God has created us? If we accept the evolutionary process of development, then the more we live out of our human energies, the more fully we will attain the next level of continued consciousness. In other words, it seems likely that we are presently in some intermediate step in evolution. By *being* our very best self, we prepare ourselves for the next steps in the journey that may well go on into infinity. What we *do*, then, in terms of jobs and successes may well be much less significant than who we are. Our ability to function out of the energies of our being may stand for us as the ultimate purpose in life. Acting in loving and free ways may, more than anything else, lead us to on-going growth and fulfillment in this life and in the lives to come.

Reducing Anxiety Through Language

We have a marvelous capacity for dramatizing life's events. We create anxiety by the way we represent certain life experiences within ourselves. We make them larger and worse and more intense than the way they really are. We represent the dentist's drill as a tool of torture. In our mind, we hear the sound of the drill increased by 100 decibels. We are sure our tooth will be pulled. So, we fill up with anxiety and fear.

Much of our dramatizing ends up in catastrophic beliefs. Once we represent the event in a catastrophic manner, within our imagination, then we will likely play out the actual event in this catastrophic way. Our internal "talk" or "pictures" tend to create the reality.

Most of us have learned to think and talk dramatically from childhood on. Teachers reinforce learning through drama. Parents create rules dramatically: "Your face will freeze like that if you keep giving me that look!" Almost all the nursery rhymes contain catastrophe. Humpty Dumpty could not be put back together again. Jack broke his head; the three *blind* mice got their tails cut off with a carving knife; London Bridges came falling down. Then the children go to bed and we say "...when the bough breaks the cradle will fall and down will come baby cradle and all. Good night." Then we turn out the light and call back: "Sleep tight; don't let the bed bugs bite."

So drama and catastrophe are peppered through our language and thought. They can create and intensify anxiety. By talking and thinking *realistically*, we counter the dramatic language and learn to represent the world in a less threatening and dangerous way.

Just because we represent certain situations as dangerous, awful, terrible, intolerable, etc. does not make them so. If we tend to become anxious in situations, it may be that we are dramatizing. Consequently, we distort the reality and respond to the distortion in anxiety.

By challenging our language and the beliefs that create anxiety, we can reduce it considerably. We have power over anxiety, if we can be open to challenging the way we see and think and talk about events that we sense endanger us. By remaining as realistic as possible in our minds, we break the catastrophic views that generate anxiety within us.

Entering our anxiety to understand it opens the door to our inner core. While anxiety does not feel comfortable, its presence reveals in an indirect and often oblique way energies that move deeply within us.

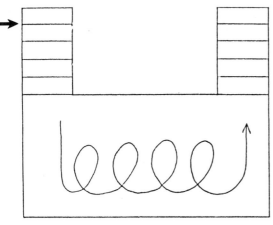

6: THE LANGUAGE OF ANGER

Anger can speak a confusing language. It rarely means what it sounds like. So we have a special task of understanding and translating anger to gain its true meaning. As children we have all doubted our parents' angry cry while punishing us: "This hurts me more than it does you." Surprisingly, the display of anger originates in energies of love, freedom, and survival. To reach those energies, we need to enter and grasp the sounds of anger.

Of all our human emotions, anger probably owns the worst reputation. From our youth we were taught, "You shouldn't get angry." "Bad" and anger got connected in our experience. Somehow only parents could get angry...or school teachers. But certainly not us. So, many of us grew up not allowing anger to surface. Others of us could not keep the lid on, and would "pitch fits" and "throw temper tantrums." Of course, we were properly reprimanded for that: "You bad child."

As with all our emotions, anger satisfies a number of useful functions. Consequently, it can serve us effectively. But it contains a hooker: anger can hurt as well, if we do not work with it. In this chapter I want to show you its functions, and then how you can work with it so that anger can work for you.

Functions of Anger

1. Anger protects us against outside threats. It works as an attack emotion. If we sense someone invading our domain, we might attack back or attack first in order to guard us from harm. The basis of paranoia lies in a person's belief that he or she stands vulnerable to the outside world, and so must attack and destroy it, before the world destroys him or her. Thus, many paranoid persons exhibit strong anger.

Although we may not be paranoid, all of us feel vulnerable at times. Perhaps I am at a party and make a comment about a movie I enjoyed. Bob responds by saying: "You liked *that* movie? That was probably the worst movie of the year. They should have paid people to go to it." The whole group laughs. I react with anger inside. I may say nothing to Bob, but I am angry. I think: "The creep. he doesn't have any sense of judgement anyway." Through my anger, I invalidate his judgement, thus protecting *my* judgement of movies. My anger worked to save me.

I might also use my anger to say something sarcastic to him and attempt to get the group to laugh at him. This way I save face. So I say: "But Bob, I've been telling you for years that you can't judge a movie as bad just because it didn't have a Road Runner cartoon with it." The group laughs, my judgment on films is safe-guarded in the group's eye, and Bob has been duly shot down.

(Now, I am not suggesting that this tactic is your most helpful approach. I only want to show you how we use anger, at times, to protect ourselves.)

Often, anger can mask our deeper self. It serves as a barrier to other people getting close to us and seeing our inner life. When we wear masks, we show others who we are not. Anger is such a mask. It blocks others from discovering us. It holds them at bay. At times keeping people away seems to be good for us. We think it works to our advantage. But it also produces a negative result. It drives people away from us.

Self-revelation, on the other hand, draws people

toward us. But self-revelation also leaves us vulnerable. Now we stand in a risky position. John tells Susan how he feels. He shares his anxiety and doubts. He stands exposed before her. Time and again, she fails to respond to him with understanding. Instead, she ignores his self-revelations. Eventually, he draws back from her and gradually anger and resentment begin to arise. Underneath the anger, he loves Susan; but to guard against too much hurt, he converts the hurt-love into anger.

Consequently, we help ourselves in the midst of our own anger to ask: "What might I be protecting?" By answering that question, we can then decide more consciously whether we want to use anger to protect us, or seek some other form of protection.

2. Anger serves as a way of proving to ourselves and others that we exist. If my children do not respond to my pleas of "Come and eat," then I do not exist for them at that moment. To prove to them I do exist, I get angry and yell. Now they know I am there.

If time and again people sense that when they talk, it means nothing to others, they may begin to doubt their own existence. By becoming angry, they prove, at least to themselves, they do exist. They feel their heart beat quicker and their blood course through their veins; their skin grows red and their body warms up. They hear their voice and feel their tears. Now they know, thanks to their anger, they still live.

When we do not feel we exist or count in the world or to someone, we experience hurt. And hurt relates directly to anger. One of the key sources of hurt and anger lies in an old childhood belief most of us have learned. This belief creates incredible internal havoc for many people. If you can unlearn it, you will literally help yourself to happiness.

The belief takes this form: If my world differs from your world, one of our worlds is invalid and must be disregarded.

We learn this awful belief very early in life. Seven year old Tony goes to bed at 8:00 P.M. Dad and Mom are reading in the living room, and at 9:00 P.M. Tony comes down the stairs and whines: "Daaady. Mooomy. I..." Dad jumps in and barks: "Tony, what in heavens name are you doing up. You get back up those stairs and get to sleep. It's late."

Tony tries again: "Yeah, but, Dad, I..."

Dad jumps up again. "No but about it young man. You get back to bed this minute. You have school tomorrow. And you need your sleep."

So Tony drags himself back up to bed. He has now learned a powerful belief, namely, when his experience is different from Dad's, Tony's does not count.

The best way to see how this belief creates hurt and anger is to picture two people as two balloons, with the same amount of air, but of differing colors.

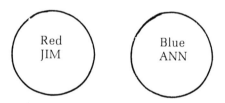

Jim says to Ann: "You really don't have much consistency in disciplining the kids." By opening his mouth and talking, Jim inflates his balloon slightly. He makes himself a little bigger than life.

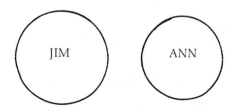

Ann's balloon has actually stayed the same size, but her experience is a psychological optical illusion, whereby she feels less than Jim. If she holds the belief that two opposing views cannot stand side by side, she is likely to *deflate* her own balloon. Now it actually does get smaller. This is the experience of hurt, to feel deflated. She can let out all the air from her balloon and feel "crushed," "destroyed," "devastated," "wiped out," etc. All the words mean hurt.

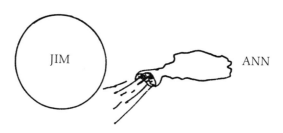

Ann has invalidated her world. She feels "just awful." She must be a lousy mother. And certainly she is a no-good person. "Jim's world is valid, mine is not."

But Ann finds it difficult to remain for long in that deflated, non-existent state. She begins blowing air into her balloon, pumping herself up. She will prove to Jim and herself that she exists. She will re-validate her world and invalidate his world. She will do it with her anger. She inflates herself, making herself larger than Jim. She reports quickly and loudly:

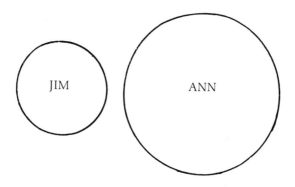

"What do you know about it? You're never home to even claim fatherhood!" In effect, she invalidates his view by claiming him to be non-existent around the house. Now, Jim can deflate in hurt or pump up in anger.

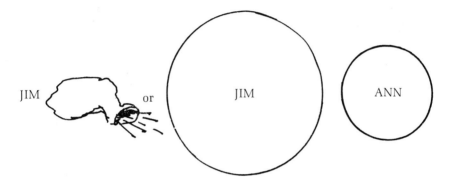

Then, it is her turn to again become hurt or more angry. But the dynamic remains the same: People experience hurt (non-existence) when they invalidate their own world or view; they become angry in their effort to invalidate the other's differing view.

Obviously, we help ourselves immensely by challenging the childhood belief that two opposing views cannot stand side by side. One must be invalidated. It would be much more useful (and I dare say more accurate) to believe: *When my world differs from yours, they both remain valid. They are only different.*

3. All of our emotions, and particularly anger, serve as an emphatic form of communication. When we feel an emotion strongly, we stand in the giving position of communication. We experience great difficulty functioning as a receiver or listener at a time of heightened feeling.

The presence of emotion signals to us our need to give or send messages. For me, anger often indicates I want my children to really get my message. I raise my voice, furl my brow and look mean. In adult communication, anger does the same. It signals a need for someone to make sure his or her message has been heard and burned forever into the soul of the receiver.

Unfortunately, while anger functions to emphatically communicate something important, it usually breaks down communication rather than enhance it. Most receivers of anger will respond in a defensive, protective way. Remember, they probably have that old belief that two opposing worlds cannot both be valid. So, they do not usually get the real message of the giver who uses anger to express him/herself.

4. Finally, anger serves at times to cover over depression. In any grieving process, the pain of the loss may be so deep, that getting angry can give some relief to the person. In other circumstances, people might remain hostile and angry, rather than sad because they prefer anger to depression. It may not feel as bad. If they stopped being hostile or irritable they might become depressed.

This also works in reverse. Some people mask anger by staying depressed. Somehow, depression in our culture seems more acceptable than anger. If I am depressed, people might come toward me in a nurturing way. If I am angry and hostile, people will move away from me. So I stay depressed and do no let others see my socially unacceptable anger.

Working With Anger

As you learn how anger works within you, hopefully you will realize that you create your own anger. You become angry due to your beliefs and responses to a situation you view as threatening your domain in some way. Certainly, if the 260 pound man had not stepped on your foot in the elevator, you would not have become irritated. But, nonetheless, what you did inside yourself in response to the foot-stepping created your anger. Once you accept your role in creating your anger, you have a good chance of working effectively with the anger.

The second awareness I would like you to have is this: Try not to label anger as good-bad, right-wrong, justifiable-unjustifiable. Accept it only as there. Especially if you tend to view anger as bad, it will become more difficult to work with than if you see it only as there. It is simply a part of your life.

Try, instead, to determine if your anger works for you or against you. "In this situation, does my anger help me or hurt me? Does it help or hurt this relationship?" If you decide it helps you, then expressing your anger directly becomes your most useful option. If you sense your anger does not help in this situation, then you can work to reduce or eliminate it.

Here we need not talk about those times our anger works for us, except to say assertive behavior will generally be the response of preference. For example, I may decide my anger will help the auto mechanic work more carefully on my car. I then need to assert myself so he understands the importance of a well-running car in my life.

On the other hand, when you decide your anger is not helpful, what can you do? Clearly, to express it directly becomes counter-productive. To remain angry and hold it inside will also not be helpful to you.

In this case, you may find it helpful to express your anger to a third party. Just saying it out loud helps sometimes. However, simply venting the anger does not dissipate it. It may feel better for a short time, but if you do not alter anything else within you, or in the situation, then your anger will return.

More effective in attempting to reduce and eliminate your anger is to realize that your beliefs and judgments about the event are causing the anger. By altering these beliefs, you will reduce the anger.

As I indicated earlier in this chapter, a key anger belief is: When my view and another's differ, one of our views is invalid. To reduce anger (and hurt) it is more helpful to hold a countering belief, namely, when my view and another's view differ, both are valid, only different.

Anger occurs when you attempt to invalidate another's view. For instance, when you say: "She should have called me about the cancellation of the meeting.

What a lousy PTA president. She should be ousted." In effect, you are saying: "The president's behavior is not valid. Her world should not have happened as it actually did happen. Thus, her world does not count to me." The anger occurs because I demand her world to be other than it is; but it is the way it is. By my demands I take away the reality of her world in my own mind. Unfortunately, her reality remains, and that keeps the anger alive.

Instead, try to realize that her reality is simply hers. She failed to call. You would have appreciated a call and did not get one. Both realities remain valid, only different.

I learned this valuable belief from a woman in therapy. She told me company had come for supper the night before. She spent the entire day cleaning and cooking, wishing to make this a special occasion. To add color to the meal she decided to prepare spinach salad.

When she served the salad, one of the woman guests impulsively blurted out: "Ugh, spinach makes me sick." The hostess felt "crushed." She went to the kitchen in tears. Then she became angry with the guest. "If she doesn't like it, why not have the manners to keep your mouth shut!" she insisted.

After a few "huffs and puffs" it dawned on her. She thought: "Wait a minute, I made that salad because I wanted to make the evening pleasant for my guests. That's a fine thing to do. My guest must have a good reason for not liking spinach. And even though I wish she would have said nothing, there are probably reasons why she responds so impulsively."

This woman validated her own position as a gracious hostess attempting to please her guests. And she validated the guest's position of spontaneously expressing her reaction to spinach. This woman taught me: In conflict, both positions are valid, only different. (I can't remember if I charged her for that session. I hope not. I should have paid *her*!)

Closely connected to this belief about two views

being valid, only different, is another set of beliefs, called the "tyranny of the shoulds" by Karen Horney. Should, musts, oughts, have to's will cause considerable anger.

Remember that little legislator inside of us who goes around making up rules for everyone and ourselves to follow. We legislate everything from the weather ("It shouldn't have rained during my vacation") to our spouses's behavior ("She should keep the house cleaner"). I legislate about stop lights when I drive. My law state that when I drive all lights should be green.

As I mentioned earlier, the problem with legislating so much lies in our lack of executive power. Most of the time, we cannot enforce our legislations. I have no power to enforce my rule about green lights. When our rules get broken, we get angry. When we cannot get the world to respond the way we insist it must, then we become angry. Interestingly, most of our legislations smack of ir-rationality. They literally fly in the face of reality.

You can observe that clearly in my rule about green lights. When I am irritating myself at the red stop light because I am insisting it must be green, I am denying reality. I refuse to accept the real world as it is. The world must be the way I demand. In fact, a red light *is* there. My insistence does not change it. My continually demanding it be green only frustrates me.

We help ourselves by challenging the laws we make demanding the world and all its inhabitants be a certain way. We can do that by realizing life is exactly as it is and not as we think it must be. Furthermore, it is the way it is for very good reasons. We simply do not know all the reasons. But because we do not know them does not mean the reasons are not there.

We can think about this in a specific way. Let's say someone insults you, and you become angry legislating inside of yourself that he should not have said that. Try challenging the law, saying: "Yes, he did say that, al-though I do not like it that he did."

And here is why he said it. If you were able to lay out

his entire life on the floor, and walk through it moment by moment, you would understand why he called you a name. You would know how he learned to attack back at age two, and how he thought and felt about people and events. You would understand the way his mind worked and how he learned to react and respond to simple and complex situations. You would see all his inner workings leading up to now when he insulted you. And when he said it, you would say: "Now that makes sense. I understand why he said that. I do not like it, but I understand it." And there would be no shoulds or oughts in your thoughts at all.

In other words, good reasons exist for people to believe as they do. Although we will never know all those reasons, we can know they exist. Based on that awareness, we can learn to lift the inner demands we place on others to behave as we insist they must behave.

On hearing this point of view, many people object: "You mean, I should just roll over and play dead. If someone wants to kick sand in my face I should let them and not become angry?"

I am not suggesting at all that we allow people to dump on us or that we do nothing in the face of real problems. If someone insults you, Problem One exists: that person's ill feeling toward you. If you respond with anger, Problem Two exists, namely your anger.

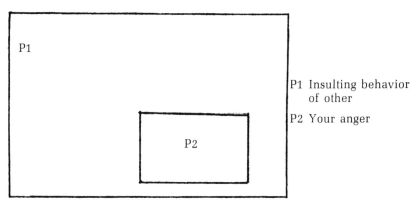

P1 Insulting behavior
of other

P2 Your anger

Now, you have two problems, the one out there and

the one inside of you. Problem Two, your anger, will most likely interfere with your efforts to deal effectively with Problem One. By eliminating or reducing Problem Two, you become freer in your ability to respond creatively to Problem One. Angry feelings do not lend themselves to creative problem solving. If you want the other person to stop insulting you, you can work hard and creatively to accomplish that without the anger. Reducing your anger, then, can actually assist you in gaining what you seek — an end to insults.

A particular belief showing up in children (and carried by them into adulthood) that creates anger has to do with *fairness*. Many of us have the rule that says "Life should be fair." Nothing could be further from reality. It would be wonderful if life were fair, and certainly we can work to make it such. But it often is not fair. Yet we keep insisting it should be so.

Actually, we usually do not really mean "fair" when we say it. I have come to recognize the practical definition of fair goes like this: Fair is that process whereby I got my way. Unfair is the process whereby I did not get my way. A man and a woman apply for the same job. She gets it. You will not hear her saying: "Gee, that was an unfair process." On the contrary, she will applaud the decision, stating: "Now that was really fair. It's about time they hired a woman." And the man is mumbling: "How unfair. The only reason she got the job was she's a woman."

When somebody talks with me about how unfair something was, I try not getting caught on equality, justice and those kind of concepts. I try, instead, to respond to the message underneath, namely, that he or she did not obtain something desired. So I might say: "I'm sorry you didn't get the job." You can bypass a lot of arguments this way, and keep yours and the other person's anger to a minimum.

Another thought that keeps anger pumped up contains the phrase "justifiable anger." I have never met a person who did not believe his/her anger was not justifiable. Of course, we think our anger is justifiable. Otherwise, we would not be angry. When we say "justifiable" about our anger, we keep it alive. In effect, we say to ourselves that we have every right to be angry and plan on staying angry for quite some time. The difficulty with this kind of thinking lies in the fallacy that two types of anger exist, justifiable and unjustifiable. In practical life, only justifiable anger is experienced by us. The more significant question has nothing to do with justification, but with usefulness. Is our anger useful to us in attaining our goals or not? By using the adjectives useful/unuseful in connection with our anger, rather than justifiable/unjustifiable, we work more practically with our anger.

One of the most helpful countering attitudes to anger is this belief: *In the great scheme of life, how important is this event?* Trying to place an event in a value or time perspective often decreases its power. As we decrease the force of the event, we may even discover humor in it. It is quite difficult to be both angry and humored at the same time.

So many conflicts in home and work settings appear insignificant in the great scheme of life's events. Often, people know the issue is minor. In marriage counseling, people will frequently introduce an issue by saying: "Now, I know this may seem like a very little thing, but..." At which point I jump in with, "But, you have made it into a gigantic issue." Keeping issues and events in perspective reduces anger and allows us more freedom to walk gracefully through life.

One last word about anger. This emotion, like all the others, serves as a signal to us of who we are deep within the core of us. Generally, it acts as an indirect and somewhat unclear signal, but a signal nonetheless. As a signal, anger is always useful. It serves us. But, to know what it signals, we help ourselves by accepting our anger simply as part of our life. I want to encourage you not to resist your anger, but to understand it and use it as a way of journeying inward to the depths of your heart.

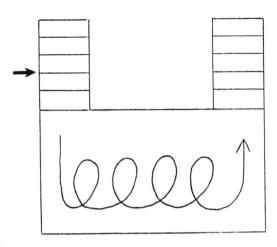

7: INNER AND OUTER VOICES

Having entered our emotions, the journey inward may proceed with vigor. In these next few chapters we will move from the surface voices of our experience to the quiet, but strong voice of our hearts.

In the scripture writings of St. Paul he once complained: "I cannot understand my own behavior. I fail to carry out the things I want to do, and I find myself doing the very things I hate...The fact is, I know of nothing good living in me — living that is, in my unspiritual self — for the will to do what is good is in me, but the performance is not...Every single time I want to do good it is something evil that comes to hand. What a wretched man I am!" (St. Paul, Letter to the Romans 7:14:24)

St. Paul's reflection demonstrates the terrible stress we all experience at times. Paul's functioning or behavior did not match up with the energies of his heart. That mismatch threw him into tension and turmoil. Confused by doing the opposite of what he desired, he could not understand what drove him.

Looking at his "misbehaviors" he drew a conclusion about himself in the form of a dramatic generalization: "I know of nothing good living in me..." Paul made a fatal mistake in judgment. He moved from assessing his behavior negatively to assessing himself negatively. He sensed, however, something good about himself, namely, the will to do good, but woe was he, his performance never (another generalization!) measured up. In effect, Paul shared with us his neurosis. He experienced a tearing apart in his life. His external self (his functioning and behavior) did not fit well with his internal self (his being or heart). The result for Paul? Inner stress and pain. "What a wretched man I am!" Paul's confession could well be spoken by most of us at times. To work with our inner tension, to attempt to move our functioning and our being into graceful harmony will now be the focus of our work.

Creation as Voices

To reach our inner word, it is helpful to view all of creation as voices. These voices speak to us in some way. They can be divided into two groups: outside voices and an inner voice.

First, let's look at the inner voice, or the voice of our heart. I believe we can more easily understand this inner voice if we accept the reality of God — a God who in some fashion created us. Ultimately, a theological belief serves as the basis of self-knowledge. This belief states: God, who is love, created us wholly good.

Theology and psychology have argued the goodness or corruptness of human nature. As a psychologist I have most dramatically experienced the fundamental goodness of every human being I have gotten to know. The processes that follow will demonstrate that optimistic point of view.

As a student of theology I have also realized the basic goodness of the human species. God, I believe, is the creative force of human and all life. In the beginning, it does not seem to me that God created things and people, then determined he did a pretty good job and decided to love what he made. Rather, accepting God as love, God, no doubt, did what God does best, which was to actively love, and the result of his loving turned out to be creation. We, then, are the effects of God's act of loving. As such effects, we stand without evil or sinfulness. What God created is wholly good and reveals, as fully as any limited creation can, the loving power of God.

While for a lot of believers the above may appear self-evident, many people do not believe this. They fail to believe that at their hearts they are fundamentally good. Some time ago, on the front page of the *Milwaukee Journal*, I read an article called "A Good Spanking?" It concerned the Moral Majority and their objection to a pamphlet on parenting put out by the U.S. Government. Specifically, they objected to the position that spanking a child is usually not an effective means of discipline. The spokesperson for the Moral Majority presented his theological view of human beings, stating "I think God knows more about child rearing than the bureaucrats. Christian theology tells us that people are born bad. They are born sinners. There is only one thing that can drive that out..." The quote ended, leaving us to speculate whether the grace of God or a good spanking drives out evil.

The government also had a theological view. In the pamphlet they wrote: "Nowadays, we know that *children are born neither good nor bad.* How they turn out depends on the strengths and weaknesses they inherit and how they get along with us and we with them." How the government knows this is beyond me.

The third theological view states: *We are born wholly good.* Certainly evil exists in the world. But at the heart of us, within our nature as human persons, lies only goodness. In our goodness we are born into a world marked by the experience of evil. We take the effects of this evil into us, so that the goodness at our heart must work through layers of good and evil.

Evil first came into the world (the original sin) because one of the powers of our nature is free will. As soon as we posit freedom we necessarily must accept both alternatives, good and evil. Perhaps the "original sin" was some choice the first creatures made in their

own evolutionary process of moving toward a fuller
human life. Due to their own evolutionary limits, they
made occasional choices that slowed down or retarded
their growth toward humanness.

As soon as a choice for lesser life was selected, "sin"
entered the world and began its continued influence.
Today, when the child is born wholly good, he/she
enters a world filled, now, with forces that will help
him/her to become more human, and other forces that
lead the child away from full human life.

At our core, then, we are loving free persons filled
with life and powers to grow and become rich and marvelous human beings. At our hearts speaks a voice. It is
the voice of God who created us, and the voice of our
nature.

The Natural Law

Another way of labeling this voice of our nature is to
call it the Natural Law. This is the law we must follow.
The natural law states "You are to be and to function as a
human being." Every bit of creation holds its own natural
law. The law of the tree states it is to be a tree. The tree
follows that law perfectly and does tree things. If it
started to meow or talk it would no longer be a tree. It
would be something else because it is not in the nature of
a tree to meow.

As human beings, we seem to be the only piece of
creation that has a *choice* to follow its law of nature or
not. We have the choice to function humanly (according
to our nature) or not. Consequently, for us, it becomes
critical to listen well to the voice of our heart (of our nature) because it tells us who we are as human creatures
and how we are to function. When we follow this inner
voice we obey our natural law and function in fully
human ways.

If the voice of our hearts was magnified and we
heard it clearly if might well reflect the words written in
the scriptures Song of Songs: "How beautiful you are my

love, how beautiful you are. You are wholly beautiful,
my love, and without blemish" (Song of Songs 4:1,7).

Now, you may be thinking I am painting much too
rosy a picture of human nature. Or that I sound like the
philosopher, Rousseau. Was it not his idea that we were
born naturally good and should be left free to act accordingly? We know his community without laws and restric-
tions never worked.

Well, I do not want to go as far as Rousseau. I believe
there is evil in the world, but not at the center of our
being. I am talking about the core of us, not about our
functioning. And there at our heart, we remain good.

So, here we are born into this world wholly good. As
soon as we arrive we begin to hear outside voices, which
speak to us loudly. Imagine, if you will, our center as a
tiny ball of rich and powerful energies. As that ball entered the world, it began to be layered over with voices
from the outside. As the ball grew it gained more and
more layers or voices. Now, some of those voices were in
harmony with the inner voice of our heart. Other voices
were in disharmony. As time went on, those outer voices
got louder, and we tended to become more and more attentive to them, and less attentive to that inner voice of
our core.

Think of it this way: The voice of our heart works
like a tiny transistor radio with very weak batteries. The
outer voices blare out to us as though coming from a giant
stereo system with four huge amplifiers, turned up to
volume 10. Obviously, we will hear those loud voices
before we recognize the transistor at our center.

For some fortunate people, many of these outside
voices will be tuned into the same channel as their inside
voice. They will experience harmony and grow up liking
who they are. They will find peace within. Others, less
fortunate, will hear outside voices in disharmony with
their inner voice. They will then deaden the inner voice,
or adjust its station to the outside voices, thereby becoming faithful to what is outside themselves rather than
who they are from within. They will generally not think

well of themselves, except insofar as they *function* suc-
cessfully in the outside world in conformity with the
voices that dictate success and acceptance.

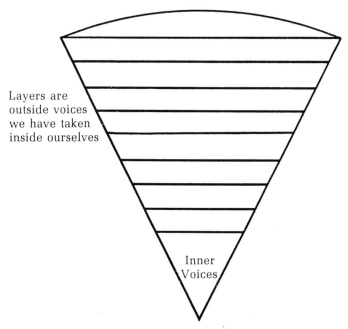

These outside voices function as *layers* that cover
over our core energies (our inner voice). Picture the
human being as a cone-shaped symbol. The inner voice
proclaims "You are beautiful, you are a lover, you are
free." The outside voices enter us and become layers in
us as we accept them throughout our life. We learn to listen to and believe these voices, some of which accurately
reflect reality, others of which do not reflect reality.
However, because we have accepted these voices within
us, we believe them all to be true and accurate reflections of the world.

When some of these voices or layers do not match
the voice of our core, we experience dissonance. Since
we do not like to stay dissonant, we tend to invalidate the
weaker voice, which is often the inner voice. We become
faithful to the layers in us rather than to our heart.

We tend to believe the layers or outer voices not because they are true, but because they are loud. Just because we believe something does not make it true. If I believe that two plus two equals five, it does not make it so. If I believe that I am not a lovable person, it does not make me unlovable. Just because people used to believe the sun went around the earth, it did not mean it happened that way.

So, within us we possess many layers that are not accurate reflections of the world, even though we continue to believe them. These inaccurate layers or voices cause dissonance. They do not match with the reality of our heart's voice.

Outside Voices

What are these outside voices we hear and take into us as true; and then turn into layers that cover our innermost voice? Well, they come from our parents, teachers, peers, churches, T.V., and all the cultural and environmental forces around us. Some of the voices we hear resonate well with our heart's voice. Examples might be:
I am lovable as I am.
Other people enjoy being with me.
No matter what I do, Dad and Mom love me.
I like helping others.
I enjoy the joys of others.
I want to make my own decisions.
These kind of voices match the voice of my heart and magnify that inner voice.
Other voices do not resonate well with our heart's voice. Examples might be:
If I speak up, people will think I am dumb.
I must never make a bad impression on others.
Others are always better than me.
People should act according to my values.
Strong feelings are wrong.
I must always do things perfectly.
These kinds of voices create dissonance with the voice of our heart. They generate stress that is often re-

solved by the denial of the inner voice.

The Dynamics of Voices

Once again, picture the human person as a cone.

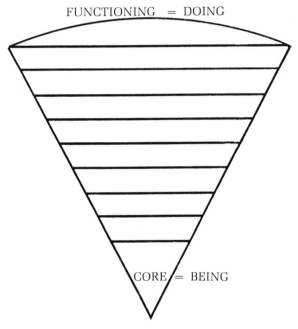

At the bottom of this cone lies the core of rich energies we possess from birth. I refer to this center as our core, heart, inner voice or energies.

These energies are layered over by all the voices and experiences we have had in life that impact us in some way. The very top layer of the cone represents our *functioning.* This layer is our *doing,* just as the core energies are our *being.* The top layer shows us to the world. People see us through our doing. This top layer consists of our *behavior,* our expressed thoughts, and our *feelings.*

Contrary to popular belief, our feelings serve as part of the external expression of ourselves. They are at the top of us, not necessarily at the heart of us. In the 60's and early 70's feelings were very much in vogue in many psychology schools. People often said things like "If you get in touch with your feelings you will know yourself." I tend not to believe that. I believe that if you get in touch with your feelings, you will know your feelings.

Our emotions live at the external edge of us. They serve as signals to the outside world as well as to our own inner life of who we are. But we are *not* our feelings. Nor are we our expressed thoughts. In other words, we are *not* our external functions. *We are not our top layer.*

Unfortunately, in our culture, many people identify who they are with what they do at that top layer of functioning. Their worth is tied to what they do or feel. They determine how good or bad they are according to the top layer of functioning. They focus their attention on the outer cover of themselves rather than on their inner core.

So, let's pull together what we have so far. At the core of us exist energies wholly good and powerful. These energies are layered over by beliefs, attitudes and experiences, some of which match our heart and some of which do not. All of our external functioning (top layer) is caused by our good energies coming up through the many layers within us. Some of these layers facilitate the movement of these energies so they come up in a pure direct way, surfacing in behavior and feelings that match our core. Other times, our good energies hit layers that retard and inhibit them. The energies, in effect, get detoured and are expressed in disconnected and ineffective ways. That is, what gets expressed in our functioning does not match our heart directly, but only indirectly and confusedly.

In other words, all that happens at the top of us (our behavior and feelings) arises from the good inner core of us, moving through the many layers inbetween. What we *do*, then, springs from our being, our nature, our center." When our behavior matches well with the energy of our heart, it means that energy came up through helpful, harmonious layers. When our behavior or feelings do not match our heart's energies, it means those energies hit debilitating layers within us, and surfaced in unclear and confused behavior.

An example of an energy coming up directly will help. We notice someone who appears sad. We go to the person and say: "I sense you are sad. Would you like to talk about it?" That is our functioning at the top layer. Our behavior is approaching that person and saying kind words. Our feeling is concern. That behavior and feeling comes from an energy deeply within us. The energy rises up directly through all the operating layers. And those layers are helping the energy surface. Some of the operating layers sound like this: "It is good to be kind to people who are sad." "She will be grateful for my concern." "She will feel better if someone understands her." "I will feel good for helping her." "It is the Christian thing to respond caringly to another."

When our hearts' energies move up in us through facilitating layers, and surface in behavior and feelings that match our heart, then we experience inner harmony. Now we are not only being human, but we are also *functioning* humanly. That leads to peace.

Let's look at the same situation, but this time with our functioning not matching our being or core. We see the sad person, but decide not to say anything and ignore him or her. Our behavior is avoidance; our feeling is some fear and uncomfortability.

The energy of our heart remains the same as in the other instance. It is an energy of love and care. That energy begins its journey upward and as it passes through facilitating layers it hits a non-facilitating layer. Perhaps it hits the layer: "I'd be embarrassed to say anything." Then it hits another: "I cannot cope with someone else crying." Our loving energy may strike against other layers, such as: "It's not my place to say anything;" "It will seem as though I am prying;" "I can't help her anyway;" and so on.

By the time our rich loving energy has come through these debilitating layers, it reaches the surface expressing itself in avoidance and discomfort. It got detoured on its way to the top. So we end up functioning in a way that fails to match clearly the energy or voice of our heart. In our heart moved loving energies; in our functioning we showed avoidance and discomfort. Now, St. Paul's complaint about doing the opposite of what he wills makes sense. He and we become stressed.

In fact, we now face the fundamental stressor in our lives, namely the conflict between our doing (top layer) and our being (energies of our heart). When the outside and inside of us do not match, we feel torn as Paul did. When we live out of sync, then we cannot remain true to our deepest self or voice. Living faithfully to the voice of our hearts is what it means to be "true to yourself."

Certainly, we find it difficult to always match our functioning to our energies. But no matter what our behavior is, I want you to know that behavior comes from a very good place in us. Anger, for instance, usually comes from the energy of love. Why do parents often get angry with their children? Because they love them. Kids do not believe it when parents say things like that because the parents' behavior does not match well with the energy of love in their hearts. The parents show irritation with the child for not brushing her teeth because they want her to care for herself. But the child only sees the irritation and draws a conclusion about the *being* of the parents: "They *are* crabs."

The parents, also, can view their irritation and draw a conclusion about their *being*: "we are *bad* parents." They are not *bad* parents because they became angry. At their core they remain loving parents who sometimes express that love in irritating and angering ways.

Friends and lovers can operate in disharmony *within* themselves and create disharmony *between* one another. We might deal with our energy of love for a friend by avoiding him or her. Why? Because that love energy may have hit a layer that says: "I do not want to come toward my friend and possibly experience rejection. Rejection is so terrible I must avoid it at all costs." We listen to that voice and choose to be faithful to the layer rather than being faithful to the energy of love at our heart. So we avoid and that leads to stress and disharmony in us and in the relationship.

We might act shyly or non-assertively. That behavior usually comes from an energy of wanting to be loved. We want to be cared for and we want others to think well of us and accept us. So, we act out of sync by functioning in a shy way, making it more difficult for others to know and care for us.

Or we might behave in a defiant manner at times. This functioning can come from the energy of freedom within us. A layer tells us the way to freedom is defiance. So we listen to that layer and act accordingly. The end result is discrepancy between our behavior and our heart.

At stake lies the issue of *integrity*. Perhaps St. Francis of Assisi would be the patron saint here. He seemed to possess a great desire to have his external behavior match consistently with his inside behavior. He wanted his behavior to reflect his spirit.

When we balance our inner and outer life, then we operate as full human beings. At these points we follow the law of our nature. And we will know peace.

But to follow the law of our nature we need to be in touch with the energies of our heart and know the layers that help and hinder these energies from surfacing in matching behavior and feelings.

Our tendency is to listen more attentively to the voices of our layers than the voice of our heart. We become faithful to the layers, committing ourselves to their directions. Sometimes, they happen to also express the message of our heart; at other times they do not. I want to encourage you to pursue and become more attentive to your inner voice that reveals your best self. As you discover that voice more fully, you will then commit yourself to it and become faithful to your own heart — and to the voice of God that speaks to you from your center.

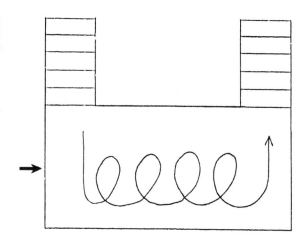

8: THE VOICE OF OUR IDENTITY

In large part, we form our identity based on the voices we hear *outside* of ourselves. We use our top layer of functioning to determine who we are. A social psychologist, Harold Kelly, helped us understand this process through his Attribution Theory of personal identity.

Kelly said that if we see people behave or feel in a certain way regularly, we eventually attribute that quality to the person. We predicate the behavior or feeling directly to the individual, linking the behavior to that person's identity. If I see my neighbor going off the the YMCA every day to swim, I eventually say "He *is* a swimmer." If I experience someone who appears angry much of the time, I say "She certainly *is* an angry person."

We do the same with people's expressed attitudes. Someone talks frequently about social issues and gets involved in them and we say: "He *is* really a committed person to social issues." Or, someone often expresses a sense of helplessness and pessimism ("Everything I touch turns out badly."), and we might conclude he or she *is* inadequate. Last year while coaching my son's basketball team, one little player kept missing lay-ups and each time he said:"I know I can't make these shots.

I'm no good." If that attitude/behavior continued being expressed in Tim's life, people would eventually attribute it to his personality; "Tim sure *is* a loser." Based on other people's top layer of functioning, we tend to attribute that functioning to their person. We conclude they are what they do.

Another social psychologist, Daryll Bem, came along and said that what we do to other people in attributing functions to their being, we also do to ourselves. We tend to form our identity based on what we do and feel. Our performance tells us who we are. If you asked me: "Dale, who are you?" I might well say "I'm a psychologist," because I see myself *doing* psychological things all day long.

I hope you can see the critical problem with forming our identity based on our functioning. When the external functioning shifts or ceases or operates imperfectly, then our identity becomes threatened. Perhaps one of the best examples of this threat to identity occurred in the 1960s during and after the Vatican Council of the Roman Catholic Church.

Many Catholics experienced a loss of identity. My mother was one of those persons. Although a liberal, she expressed to me that she did not feel like a Catholic anymore. She was not quite sure who she was religiously. It became difficult for her to know what it meant to *be* a Catholic anymore because so many *behavors* and *beliefs* Catholics held dear were changing.

How did Catholics know they were Catholic 20 or 30 years ago? How did they identify themselves as Catholic? Well, they *behaved* as Catholics did. They went to mass and communion on Sunday and confession every Saturday. They did not eat meat on Fridays. They fasted during Lent. And they played bingo.

They also believed certain things, such as the pope was infallible; the Roman Church was the one true church and a Catholic could not take part in another denomination's worship. They believed in saints, and the central role of the Blessed Virgin in prayer and devotion.

These beliefs and behaviors told people they were Catholics. Then came Vatican Council II and many beliefs and behaviors (the top layer) of the Church changed. Confession became less frequent and hot dogs were allowed on Fridays. The pope no longer seemed so infallible and Catholics began attending Lutheran weddings! It became difficult to feel like a Catholic when all these behaviors were changing.

Although, we tend to form our identity on these external functions and voices, more often than not this process is not helpful to the formation of our own identity. In fact, if we base our identity on that top layer, we will cause considerable trouble for ourselves. If we are good people based on that top layer of functioning, then all our behaviors, feelings, and expressed thoughts must be very, very good ones. If we make a mistake, act irritably, feel depressed, or get confused, then our identity may waiver.

We begin to make judgments about our whole self simply because our top layer might misfire once in awhile. When we do that, our top layer (or functioning) then controls our lives. Furthermore, when we focus our identity on our functioning, we become very dependent on other people's reaction to our behavior. If they like what we do, then we are OK; if they do not like what we do, then we are not OK. For example, I might determine my worth according to my ability to give a lecture. If the audience reaction was to yawn and sleep through the talk then I would say I am a lousy speaker. With little difficulty, I could then conclude: "And *I* am not good."

Thus, basing our identity on our functioning eventually leads to dependency on other people's reactions to us. That type of dependency will generally leave us in a threatened position. I must always *do* well, so that you will like me, which will allow me to like myself. We look for our identity in the wrong place when we rely on our functioning. Our identity lies in our core where our energies flow toward the good.

One of the first jokes I ever learned as a child makes

this same point. One night a man was on his hands and knees under a lamp post looking for something. A second man approached and asked: "What are you looking for?"

The first man replied: "I lost a dollar."

The second man asked: "Where did you lose it?"

"About two blocks down the alley."

"Well, why are you looking here?" queried the second man.

"Because the light is so much brighter here," responded the first man.

Although as an adult the joke no longer seems that funny, it does say what I want: Although our top layer may seem easier to see, it does not mean that our functioning is the place to look for the treasure of ourselves. Our identity is at our heart, and our search for it works best when we move away from our functioning and concentrate instead on our being and inner energies.

Focusing

In order to get to our heart, we will want to learn to focus. We will attempt to pay less attention to our outside, and learn how to center on and enter our inside. To focus on our core and away from our functions demands discipline.

In the last several years, many people have been disciplining themselves physically through jogging, exercise and dieting. We have been learning discipline of our bodies. Hopefully, we can learn, also, the discipline of our psyche. Presently, it is probably quite accurate to suggest that many of us are psychologically quite flabby. Consequently, we focus on whatever grabs our attention. We focus on the loud voices — past hurts, future worries, angers, failing experiences, and so on. Once we lock in on those voices, it becomes difficult to hear any others.

Regarding our identity, we actually have the choice to focus on our behavior and feelings, or to focus on our center, the seat of rich energies. We can use our functioning to decide who we are, or we can use our heart to decide our identity. It is our choice. I am my functions or I am my energies. I would strongly urge you to focus on your energies and believe you are your energies. You are not your behaviors. You are not your feelings.

Our commitment, then, is to our heart. Our first faithfulness is to the energies within us. We do not commit ourselves to the structures around us, nor to the outside voices. We commit ourselves to our own hearts. We are faithful to our deepest and best selves. And in that faithfulness, we can commit ourselves to God and others.

Perceive Rather Than Judge

Since we tend to judge persons (and ourselves) on performance, we help ourselves by trying to slow down the judging process. Two key mental processes we all use are *perception* and *judgment*. Both are vital to us and work together. Let's see how.

As I drive down the street, another driver makes a quick right turn immediately in front of me. I perceive all of this. I notice it. Based on that perception, I make a quick judgment about the driver. My judgment is: "What a jerk!"

Here is what happened: Through my perceptive powers I gained a little information. Since I need a certain larger amount of information in order to respond, I fill in the lack of information by interpreting and judging the driver. I saw him do a quick right turn into traffic and I fill in the rest, namely, "Only jerks do things like that."

But let's say I continue to perceive the situation, thus increasing my information. I drive up alongside his car and notice his left arm is in a cast. I now have more information, so I will supply a little less interpretation. I might conclude: "It must be more difficult for him to drive with a broken arm. That explains why he swung out into traffic like that. But the jerk shouldn't be driving with a broken arm!"

As I drive closer to him, I see that he not only has a broken arm, but also a gash in his forehead. I see blood streaming down the side of his face. My perceptions have given me even more information, thus allowing me to interpret less and judge more accurately. I judge: "The poor man is hurt and in need of help." Note he is no longer a "Jerk."

Finally, the man pulls his car over to the curb, and I pull in behind him. He gives me more information: "Oh, thank you for stopping. I'm trying to get to the emergency room at the hospital. I lost my balance and fell against the refrigerator and hurt my head. No one was around, so I had to try driving myself. I can't do very well because of my broken arm."

With all that information, I do very little interpreting and make my judgments more benign and gentle. From deciding he was a jerk to driving him to the hospital is a quantum leap in judgments. Generally, the less information we have, the more interpretation we will supply. We fill in the missing blanks in order to make a judgment. Our judgments will change the more information we gain, because our interpretation will decrease. The more we perceive, the less powerful and negative will be our judgments. The less we perceive, the greater the chances of harsh and negative judgments.

Applying this principle to our own identity, we can make a very important move in self-kindness. If I look only to my top layer of behavior and feelings in order to judge who I am, then I use very little information and must fill in with a lot of interpretation. My concluding judgment about myself will likely be harsh and negative.

For example, I perceive myself knocking down a crystal vase while dusting. I quickly fill in the missing blanks (most of this interpreting is automatic and unconscious) and come to the dramatic conclusion: "Dale, you idiot! You clumsy ox!"

If I understood more about me (perceived more

fully) I would not be so harsh in my judgment. I was dusting out of my care for my family. My large motor skills were perhaps never developed. I wanted to please my wife. The energy at the core of me was love. By perceiving these other layers in me and the energy of my heart, my judgment of self might be much more kindly: "I am a loving person trying to do a loving thing who made a mistake."

Perceiving ourselves and others without judging who they *are* by what they *do* was taught by the gospel story of the woman caught in adultery. This incident may well have been Jesus' fourth temptation.

The Pharisees saw themselves as the interpreters and judges of the law. They brought the woman to Jesus. Nowhere in the story is there any hint that the woman did not commit adultery. The behavior apparently occurred. The Pharisees wanted Jesus to make a judgment about what the woman did: "Master, what do you judge about this woman?"

Jesus, meanwhile, diddled around in the sand. He perceived the woman, the charges against her, heard all the details. But he kept right on perceiving, probably sensing the many layers in her life which led to this behavior. And perhaps he also sensed the goodness of her heart.

So far, no judgments, only perceptions. Then he commented: "Anyone here who does not possess debilitating and harmful layers within themselves, let them make the first judgement." Of course, everyone walked off, and Jesus went back to doodling in the sand. He made no harsh judgement regarding her, but then did offer some friendly advice: "Go and work against those debilitating layers within you." No judgments; simply perceptions about what leads to life and fullness.

Certainly we need to make judgments in order to function. But to make judgments about our *being* based solely on our *doing* will eventually cause us considerable difficulty. The more we perceive our entire self, all the way to our core, the less likely we will judge ourselves harshly.

Once we can free ourselves from using our top layer of behavior as the full source of our identity, we can then find out who we really are. The top layer is extremely helpful to us, but it only serves as the starting point of self-worth.

Our behaviors and feelings (top layer) stand as *signals* of our heart. As signals, they become very helpful to us. We often view pieces of our behavior or certain feelings as bad or awful; but as signals they are always good. Our behavior and feelings serve as the voices we hear first in our journey inward in pursuit of the voice of our heart. Since they speak to us loudly and clearly, we help ourselves by attending to them, not as statements about our whole identity, but as signals to help us know who we are. Sometimes these signs function as direct signals of our heart; at other times they stand as indirect signals. But, nonetheless, all our behaviors and feelings swing open as doors to our inner selves.

With this theory and understanding in hand, we can enter more deeply the U-process. We know our feelings and our behaviors. We know we are *not* those layers. We know there are rich and good energies deep within us; and that these energies form the basis of our self-esteem and identity.

Now our work is to journey from the top layer of feeling and behavior through all the layers of our lives to the core where our being dwells.

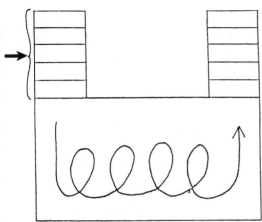

9: REACHING THE HEART: A STRUCTURED APPROACH

Two ways of journeying to our heart open before us: a more structured and less structured approach. In this chapter, I want to share with you the more structured, and usually more cognitive approach.

Think of this journey as starting at the top of you, and proceeding layer by layer downward until you hit the core.

Behavior — Feelings

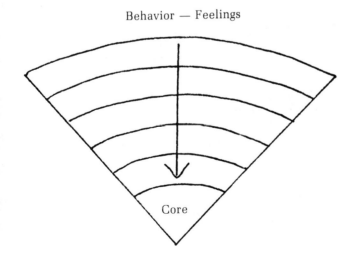

Core

The best way to grasp the process is to see it in action. To accomplish this I want to share an example of the process in my own life.

At the top of me, my feeling is impatience and my behavior is sharp speech with my children. These serve as the starting points of my journey inward, and as indirect signals of some powerful, rich, and good energy at my heart. I know these are indirect signals because I cannot immediately sense from what good place in me those inpatient feelings arise.

The first question I ask myself is "Why? Why are you feeling impatient and speaking sharply to your children?" This question simply gives me information about what is happening. My answer is: "Because my children are fooling around while brushing their teeth, taking a lot of time." I write this response on the first line under the top layer of my diagram (see figure). With this first question, then, I try to give an understanding of what triggers the feeling and behavior.

Once I have that information, then I ask: "Why is that important to me?" Repeating this question will eventually lead me to my heart. Let's continue.

"Why is it important for me to not have the children fool around while brushing their teeth?"

My answer which I write into the next layer: "Because they should go to bed promptly when we tell them to."

Third question: "Why is it important that the children go to bed promptly?"

Answer: "So I can go downstairs and have a quiet evening with Joelyn (my wife)."

Fourth question: "Why is it important for me to have a quiet evening with Joelyn?"

Answer: "Because I'm "on" all day attending to everyone's needs and now I can be "off.""

Fifth question: "Why is it important for me to be "off" in the evening?"

Answer: "So I can relax."

Sixth question: "Why is it important for me to

Because my children are fooling around while brushing their teeth; they are taking a lot of time.

Because they should go to bed promptly when we tell them to.

So I can go downstairs and have a quiet evening with Joelyn.

Because I'm "on" all day attending to everyone's needs and now I can be "off."

So I can relax

Because if I don't relax, I get worn out and cannot be as helpful to other people at work, not as responsive to my children.

Because my kids need my love.

Because I want them to grow up to be fully alive people.

Because I love them and want what is best for them.

LOVE

relax?''

Answer: "Because if I don't relax, I get worn out and cannot be as helpful to other people at work, nor as responsive to my children."

At this point I have an option. I can either pursue "helpfulness to others" or "responsiveness to my children." I chose the latter.

Seventh question: "Why is it important for me to be responsive to my children?"

Answer: "Because my kids need my love."

Eighth question: "Why is it important *for me* that my children receive my love?"

Answer: "Because I want them to grow up to be fully alive people."

Ninth question: "Why is it important for me to have them be fully alive people?"

Answer: "Because I love them and want what is best for them."

Tenth question: "Why is it important to me that I love my children and want what is best for them?"

Answer: "It just is, that's all!"

No answer really exists for the tenth question. It simply *is* that way; that is, it is according to my nature of love. When I reach this point, when I cannot go on any further, then I have most likely hit the core of me. I have reached an energy of my heart, namely love.

At the bottom of Figure 5, I write the word *love* or *caring*. At the top of me is impatience and sharp speech; at the heart of me is love. Does that top layer match the energy at my heart? Obviously, it does not. In fact, it almost appears opposite of loving care.

If I focus too much on my impatience I can conclude that I am an inadequate parent. If I focus on the loving energy of my heart, then I am a loving parent who became impatient. The difference in perspective is amazing. Staying focused on the top layer leads to self-hatred. Centering on the energy of our hearts leads to re-vitalizing those energies and acting out of them.

Just to complicate things a little, I could have gone

down another track, one that would put me in touch with a different energy at my core. My impatience over my children's brushing behavior also leads to my awareness that I desire to be free from all responsibilities at times. This leads to the core energy of freedom. I want to be free. I want to have choices to determine my own life. Is this energy of freedom a good energy? Is the energy of love good? They are great. Wonderful. But the feeling that comes out is impatience. The behavior is sharp speech. Do I like that? No, I do not. This behavior and feeling do not match well with my core love and freedom. So I do want to work at correcting the top layer, so it matches up better with my heart. Like St. Paul, I want to *do* what I *desire* (energy) to do.

But I am not a bad or inadequate person because my top layer does not match up with my heart. I am *always* a good person because I am my energies. I am love and freedom. I am, then, a very good person with powerful rich energies of love and freedom, who sometimes acts impatiently.

I hope you get a feel for what I have just done. I may have made it sound very simple in the example. But I realize this is not always so. Sometimes we can become easily stuck in journeying through our layers. I have found that it is oftentimes more helpful to work through this process with a partner. Having someone else ask the questions seems to keep us on track more easily.

I served as my wife, Joelyn's, partner using this structured approach. That dialog follows:

Dale: Joelyn, I would like you to give me some feeling that you presently have.

Joelyn: Worry.

Dale: Okay, so worry is the top layer. Now, I'll just ask the questions and you respond to them.

Joelyn: Fine.

Dale: The first question is a why question. We're just looking for information. Why are you or why have you been worried?

Joelyn: I have been worried the past couple days, in

particular, about the quality of our children's education.
Dale: Okay, and what is it about the quality of
education that you worry about?

Joelyn: I'm not sure that the school system is giving
them enough to meet what I think they're going to need
for the rest of their life.

Dale: Okay. Now the next questions are all
why-is-it-important questions. So, why is it important
that the school system give them what they need for the
rest of their lives?

Joelyn: Well, first of all, because if the school doesn't
give it to them, I'm not sure where they're going to get
this good education.

Dale: And why is it important *for you* for the kids to
get a good education.

Joelyn: I don't feel they'll be successful without that
good education.

Dale: Why is it important for you for them to be
successful?

Joelyn: Well, I think being successful will probably
ensure them of a very comfortable life in the future.

Dale: All right. And why is it important for you for
them to be comfortable?

Joelyn: Well, because I love them and it's important
to me, because I love them so much, to see that they're
comfortable and well set up in life.

Dale: Okay. And why do you love them?

Joelyn: Because they're my children.

Dale: Actually, there probably isn't much of an
answer to that. You kind of laughed when you said,
"Well, because they're my children." And that tends to
imply that you're at the bottom, or at the center of
yourself, which means that the energy at your center is
love.

Here is another example:

Dale: Can you think of another feeling or behavior
you could work with?

Joelyn: Well, since the season is winter, and a
particularly bad one, I've been feeling a lot of irritability.

Dale: Okay, good. So the top layer, the feeling, is irritability and you're already telling us a little bit about the why. It's because it is winter in Milwaukee.

Joelyn: And I feel caged in the house.

Dale: So, the why question, the factual layer underneath the feeling is I feel caged in the house in wintertime.

Joelyn: Right.

Dale: The next set of questions then is the why-is-that-important questions. Why is it important for you not to feel caged in the house in the wintertime?

Joelyn: I feel very bored when I'm faced with the prospect of being in the house day after day in the winter.

Dale: And why is it important for you not to feel bored?

Joelyn: I don't like to be bored.

Dale: Uh huh.

Joelyn: I don't enjoy the sameness of an exact routine from day to day.

Dale: And why is important for you not to have the same routine every day?

Joelyn: Well, it goes back to the irritability and the boredom, I think.

Dale: In other words, when you're doing the same thing then you get bored?

Joelyn: Right.

Comment: All right. Now, we're going back into a circle here. One of the things that happens, at times, in going through the process is that we can cycle back to one of the top layers. So we just have to stay with it and see if we can get underneath that.

Dale: You do not like the sameness because you don't like to be bored.

Joelyn: Right.

Dale: So, I'm going to ask it again. Why is it important not to be bored? Why is that important *for you*?

Joelyn: Well, when I am bored I become very restless and when I'm restless I tend not to be able to

complete my tasks. I flit from on task to another.
      Dale: Okay.
      Joelyn: I don't find a sense of accomplishment when
I don't complete the tasks.
      Dale: So, you're giving us a couple of layers. One is I
get restless and tend not to complete things. And
underneath that, the next layer down is, I don't have a
sense of accomplishment.
      Joelyn: Right.
      Dale: Now, why is it important for you to feel a sense
of accomplishment?
      Joelyn: Well, I think maybe I've been brought up to
feel that my worth, in some ways, is measured by what I
accomplish. A task completed well means I've done a
good job for the day and I'm a pretty worthwhile person
today.
      Dale: And why is it important for you to feel
worthwhile about yourself?
      Joelyn: If I don't feel worthwhile about myself, I
don't like myself. I'm miserable with myself.
      Dale: And why is it important for you not to feel
miserable?
      Joelyn: Well, if I'm not at peace with myself, I think
I'm a pretty unhappy person.
      Comment: If you could see Joelyn now, she is making
a face suggesting her last response was not much of an
answer. As she gets closer to her center, it becomes more
difficult to answer the question. Her deeper layers are
made up of long-standing, mostly unconscious, beliefs
she uses daily. She operates out of them, but does so
habitually and without awareness.
      Dale: Joelyn, what you are saying now is that you
don't want to be miserable. You want to be at peace with
yourself.
      Joelyn: Right.
      I could ask the why question again, and would get a
response like, "It's just part of human nature to want to
feel happy with yourself." This is a good signal Joelyn is
reaching her center. The energy I sense in her is that of

fullness.

Joelyn wants to be whole and as satisfied with herself and her life as possible. That movement toward the *fullness of life* is a rich and wonderful energy within her.

Briefly, I want to highlight some of the pitfalls to watch for in using this more structured process. First of all, if our feelings come up in us so intensely, it will be very difficult to calmly go through this process and enter the depth of our heart. Thus, we may need to release the strength of the feelings and settle down before attempting to journey inward.

Second, we may not know what we are looking for in our journey. We are in search of rich, good, and powerful energies that lead to life for us and others. If we stop short of reaching these energies, we have not gone deeply enough. Keep going.

Third, sometimes we will find it difficult to answer the why-is-that-important question, but we sense that we have not yet touched bottom. Then reverse the question, asking it negatively. For instance: "What would happen if what you value was taken away?" Or, in Joelyn's case, if she could not answer, "Why is it important for you to feel a sense of accomplishment?", then ask: "What would happen if you failed to accomplish something you set out to do?" That will give you a new layer.

Fourth, some people may fear what they will discover if they go inside themselves deeply. They fear discovering a core of evil or rottenness, while others fear they will discover emptiness. I assure you the journey to your heart will always end by touching a positive life-giving energy.

Fifth, keep the focus on yourself. Always ask: why is this important *for me*? Do not concern yourself with its importance for your children or friend or civilization. Why was it important *for Joelyn* that the children learn a lot in school? Not why was it important for *the children* to learn a lot in school. Keep the focusing process on *your* journey to *your* heart.

Try this process, writing it down from the beginning, and if possible, working it through with a friend or a spouse. As you get the sense of it, you will be able to work through it quickly and easily.

Now we turn our attention to the less structured process.

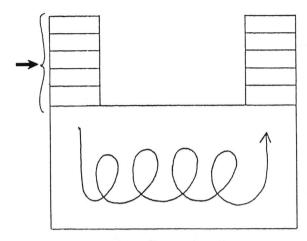

10: REACHING THE HEART: A LESS STRUCTURED WAY

When we attempt to reach our hearts in this less structured approach, the main principle to follow is this: *Enter whatever you experience.* Do not fight against or resist anything you sense within yourself. If you feel sad, for example, enter the sadness. Go toward it, allowing yourself a fuller experience of the sadness. The deeper you enter the feeling you experience, the more likely you will pass through it and exit out the other side. You will then come into a new level of experience. You enter that level and gradually pass through to the next level and so on until you finally reach your heart.

Perhaps the best way to explain this process is by demonstrating it. Since the process itself is quite non-verbal and more experiential than cognitive, it can be difficult to describe. But I will try. Recently, I wrote down the procedure as I went through it.

This was a Wednesday morning. I got up at 6:30 A.M., showered, shaved, dressed. I came downstairs, put on the coffee and went into my den. The children were not up yet, so the house was still quiet. I sat in my chair and asked myself the starting question: "Dale, who are you today?" Then I let myself simply pay attention to whatever I began experiencing.

If I feel tired, then I began with tiredness. If I feel

nervous, I start there. If I sense calm, then that becomes the beginning point. If, as I sit, I become aware of the wind blowing outside, then I enter my awareness of the blowing wind outside. So, whatever comes to me serves as the starting point. I enter that initial voice that will lead to my heart.

Now, as I asked the question, "Dale, who are you?", I was aware only of myself sitting there without being conscious of anything else. I tried to enter "just sitting there." What is it like to be just sitting? How does it feel? I wanted to allow myself to simply experience just sitting. As I continued to sit for the next 30 seconds, I began to feel some frustration. I sensed myself not going down into myself. I did not have a sense of touching anything and I wanted to.

So, I then entered my frustration. As I experienced that more fully, I had an image of banging my head against a wall. I entered that image and sensed even more fully banging and banging my head against the wall. Then I began to feel some pressure to come up with something because that night I was giving a talk about this process and wanted a good example.

At that time I began feeling empty. Nothing seemed to be moving within me. I was getting nowhere. So, I entered the emptiness. At a point like this, it becomes important to believe that whatever I am feeling will help lead me to my heart. Even when the experience seems negative, as it did here, it will lead me deeper into my center.

So I felt this void and emptiness. The word "hollow" came to me. I entered it. I realized I wanted to give something worthwhile to the people I was to address that night, but there seemed nothing to give. As I entered that awareness, I began to feel sad, a sort of helplessness. I entered the sad helplessness. Then I sensed a loss of energy and then a loss of vitality. I was feeling life draining out of me.

As I entered this sense of a loss of life, I noted a small flip inside of me. Up until now all my feelings and

senses seemed negative. But I became aware of a
nurturing element present in me, a sense I needed to
care for myself. If I was "dying" I needed to nurse myself
to well-being. I became aware how I tend, so often, to be
in a giving position and do not receive much from others.
My job and parental lifestyle demand a lot of giving. I
needed to receive life too.

I then sensed a nurturing toward myself. A
gentleness came over me, so I entered it. In staying with
that gentle nurturing, I became aware of a loving energy
in me. I entered it and stayed there. If felt good.

As I touched my heart I attempted to stay dissociated
from the object of my energy. In this case *I* was the object
of my nurturing love. I did not at this point want the focus
on the "me," but on the loving energy. I just tried to sense
the lovingness, the flow of that energy. I remained with
that movement of energy for 30 to 40 seconds. Then I
concluded: "Dale, you *are* a nurturer today." Remember,
at the beginning of this I asked who I was. Well, here was
the answer. I am a nurturer. I am my energy. When I
started I felt frustrated. That led me to my heart. I am a
nurturer. Whether I *do* nurturing things today is not the
point. The realization is that at my heart I am a nurturer.
That is who I am. Certainly, I will then attempt to
function according to the energy of my heart. I will
attempt to do nurturing things. But if I do not always
succeed, I do not stop *being* a nurturing person.
Nurturance is in my core, in my very nature.

Let's pause in this process for a moment. A couple
other pieces can be added to this dynamic, but the
central element is realizing the energy at our heart. I will
discuss the other elements shortly. However, I want to
reinforce the fundamental dynamic in this process,
which is to deeply enter whatever comes. Whether your
feelings and senses are comfortable or painful, keep
entering them.

This entering process can end right here. I am in
touch with my center and that is sufficient to give me
energy to function in human ways. However, for those

who blend a spiritual life with their psychological life, more can be done. This process can become a profound prayer form.

U-Process As Prayer

In the U-process described above, the spirit of entering whatever voices we hear predominates. That spirit continues as the process becomes prayer. People pray with great difficulty when they *fight* against outside voices. Everything they feel or sense needs to be heard as a voice telling them something of their hearts and of God.

Consequently, in this form of entry and prayer, there can be no distractions. Everything becomes part of the process. Oftentimes, people try to free themselves from distraction to focus on God. I suggest they allow anything and everything to enter their awareness because those "distractions" really are voices that will lead them to the experience of self and God at their hearts.

Now, how is this entry process a prayer form as well as an experience of our being? Basically God is known primarily from *inside* our own nature. The primary source of God's revelation is our own heart. All else is secondary revelation. The bible, churches, other people and sunsets reveal God as outside voices, one step removed from our own inner experience. Real knowledge of God, in a biblical sense, is experiential in nature. The experience of our own inner life, then, is critical in experiencing God.

Thus, when I know myself at my heart, I know the experience of God. Through the U-process above, I knew the energy of nurturing within me. I now know experientially God, the nurturer, as well. That *is* the experience of God. I do not have to talk of it, or have someone tell me about the nurturing God. I know the nurturing God from inside my own nurturing energy. God, the Creator, has created this powerful, rich energy within me, and by it reveals himself to me. I know God by knowing who I am in my energies.

This is the moment of worship. I have now encountered God. When I touch my loving energies, I know *God* who is love. When I sense my freedom, I know the loving freedom of *God* and his choice of me. When I enter *my* fullness and sense of wholeness, I then experience the creative power of *God* filling up the universe with his love. And when I grasp the energy within *me* to belong and be loved, then I touch the passion of *God* to be part of our lives.

I know these realities of God from within the experience of my own heart. Then, the voices from outside of me can confirm what I already know. If they magnify the voice of my heart, then I want to attend to them; if they do not speak in harmony with the messages of my core, I want to "de-power" them, for they do not speak of my goodness or of God.

I want to return, now, to the example I shared of entering my nurturing self. If I choose, I can now turn consciously to God. I need not specifically and deliberately turn to God. I have already done so by entering my center. But for religious-minded people we may find it helpful to our prayer to do so.

I have become aware of myself as a nurturer. I then affirm that energy in me by saying: "Dale, I am a nurturer and I appreciate that. I celebrate who I am and affirm that energy. I embrace my nurturing." After that I say: "And, now, I also know you, God, the Nurturer."

Someplace in the back of my consciousness, I know that nurturing energy is directed toward me. I need to nurture me. I try then, without forcing anything, to connect my experience to some scriptural element. I become aware of St. Luke's Gospel and his portrayal of Jesus going away alone to be nourished. So I pick up that Gospel and read some of those sections to help me magnify the voice of my heart to care for myself as Jesus did.

Thus, I have made the conscious connection between the energy of my heart and the experience of God. Keep in mind, though, that this connection is a "heady" one.

The real experience of God already came in the moment of touching and celebrating who I discovered myself to be at my heart.

A Second Example

You will best enter this process by sensing its movement. Examples serve us most effectively. I feel slow and tired. I enter the slowness and become aware of how late I got to bed last night. My wife, Joelyn, and I had been out playing tennis, eating ice cream and talking. I entered that experience and sensed my love for her. I let myself enjoy the feelings of love. I then felt a desire to do more with her. I entered that longing. Then I began feeling torn because today was a work day and I had to go to the office; but I wanted to be with her. I entered that tearing feeling. I gradually became aware that I work, in part, so that we can do more together. I sense myself as one who gains resources for Joelyn and my children. I then had a sense of being a provider. As I entered "providerness" I tried to let that energy flow over and through me.

As a provider I experienced protecting my family, giving them security and standing with them. I felt a slight tingling in my arms. I then found myself saying: "Dale, today you are a provider." I embraced that about myself and affirmed it in me. Then I moved consciously to God, the Provider. I then knew His kind caring for me. I recalled the passage in Scripture that magnified this voice of provider — the lilies of the field. So, I knew me the provider and God the Provider.

In the next chapter I will discuss with you what to *do* with our energies. Right now, the key is simply to get in touch with who we are and then be willing to stay with it. Do not try to get practical too quickly. This is a U shaped process, and not a V shaped process. Right now we have touched the bottom of the U. Do not try to come up too fast.

In sharing this process with you, it may appear to

move along very quickly and smoothly. As you begin this process it may, however, seem more difficult and take more time. Because I have been doing it almost daily for several years, I find it can take as little as three minutes and generally flows rather smoothly. In starting, however, you do need some patience. And, also, you might begin by going through the process with someone else. Your companion's job is to help you stay focused.

The U-Process With A Friend

Let me show you an example of how I worked with my wife as she entered herself. We taped recorded this account and have transcribed it as it happened.

Dale: Okay, Joelyn, I would like you to just get quiet and relaxed, and let whatever comes into your mind or your feelings come. Don't resist anything. Just try to get into the spirit of entering. Share with me whatever your very first awareness is and we'll go from there.

Joelyn: Well...I guess my feeling right now is one of restlessness. A little antsiness.

Dale: Okay, just try to enter into the antsiness. As you experience feeling antsy, kind of take me along on the journey. Let me know what you're experiencing.

Joelyn: Well, I think...I think, the antsiness comes from feeling tired right now. Or maybe a little lazy and yet I know that I have a lot of things that I really want to accomplish before the end of the day. Yet, it's tough for me to get up the energy to do these things that I know should be done. And still, I feel this urgency to do these things.

Dale: So let yourself enter the conflict between feeling sort of lazy and tired, and at the same time, wanting to get some things done today. See where that takes you.

Joelyn: Now I don't enjoy the feeling of conflict. I don't enjoy knowing I should be doing things and yet, not wanting to do them. I feel the pressure in this conflict.

Dale: Just keep entering the conflict even though it

doesn't seem enjoyable. Keep experiencing it. See where it takes you.

Joelyn: The conflict makes me resent the things I have to do because none of them are actually for me. And it's harder to get at those things because I know that they're for committees. And, you know, housework, ironing. Nothing of pleasure, really.

Dale: So the conflict is between unattractive things and doing something for yourself or your own satisfaction.

Joelyn: Right.

Dale: Okay. Again, keep trying to stay with that and maybe try now to move a little bit toward the side of doing something for your satisfaction. Try entering into that and see what that feels like.

Joelyn: Well, the things I would do around the house for my satisfaction still produce in me the feeling of restlessness. I could sit down and read. But I know the children would bring a Richard Scary book and then I would be reading to them. I could also sit and do needlework, but inevitably, when I sit down to do that, someone needs something.

Dale: So even if you do things around here for yourself, you're still doing things for others. I mean, you really wouldn't be able to do something just for you.

Joelyn: I don't feel I would at this time of the day. No.

Dale: Well, keep entering that part of you that wants to do something for you and see what that feels like and where that leads you.

Joelyn: All right. The part of me that wants to do something for me says it's Sunday. Give yourself a break. What are fun things to do? I feel like I could overcome my weariness if I could think of something that I would enjoy before I accomplish some tasks I don't enjoy. But just thinking of something I might like to do could motivate me to get the unpleasant task done, I suppose.

Dale: Just try entering that part of you that would like to go and do something for you. What does that feel like and where is it carrying you. Keep trying to enter it.

Joelyn: The part of me that wants to do something for me ... I would feel good about doing something for me.

Dale: Do you have a sense of what that something is?

Joelyn: I think maybe I could just enjoy taking a walk. It's kind of wet outside to take a walk though. Maybe go to a shopping plaza and look in all the store windows and see what the new spring fashions are. Just enjoy some time by myself.

Dale: Okay, now try entering time by yourself. Enjoying time by yourself.

Joelyn: Well, when I think of enjoying time by myself, the walk around the shopping plaza sounds as good as looking in the store windows. Maybe I'm not as tired as I think I am. I would enjoy a walk. It would feel good. I would feel carefree taking a walk.

Dale: Now, enter into the carefree and try to get an experience from inside of you of the carefreeness and see what that's like and what that feels like.

Joelyn: The image that comes to my mind with carefree is of taking off a heavy winter coat. I would take off some of these responsibilities I have and just wander around in my shirtsleeves. You know? Just be myself for a little bit.

Dale: Now you're getting to one of the core energies. The energy of freedom. And it's coming out for you in being carefree. Try to get a sense of that carefreeness and then try to just let yourself know that is who you are. At your heart, you are already carefree. You may not be acting in a carefree way, but the longing in you indicates you already are what you long to do.

Now, simply try to dwell in your carefree energy. See if you can affirm that in you and tell yourself that is who you are. And then celebrate you as a carefree person.

Joelyn: (She nods her head affirmatively.)

Dale: Can you now consciously connect to the carefree God?

Joelyn: When I think of God as spirit, as

unencumbered by all the body things, then I think we're lucky God is a spirit. If, at my heart is carefreeness, God must be like the spirit of me being unencumbered of all responsibilities. I know I like to fulfill the responsibilities eventually, but...I never thought of it before...I suppose for me to be carefree is my closest contact with God.

Dale: Exactly. As you touch your heart and your own experiences, then within you, you also know the experience of God.

This, then, has been Joelyn's process. Her journey inward began with restlessness and ended in a carefree heart.

A few comments on what Joelyn did and the dynamics of the process. Near the beginning she felt conflict and I encouraged her to keep entering it. Try not to avoid anything that comes in, even if it feels comfortable. It holds an important message.

A little later, she still seemed stuck in the conflict. One side of her felt urgency to do some things at home, and the other side of her wanted to get out for a walk. By asking her to consider the more positive side of the conflict (going for a walk) I was inviting her to get unstuck. It is helpful to make a decision to focus on one of the sides of a conflicted, ambivalent issue in order to get off the stuckness. Generally, you move off dead center in this process by choosing to focus on the more positive aspect.

A few cautions in going through this process: Stay with it. Patience is needed. Often people give up if they feel stuck. Sometimes you will reach your heart almost immediately. Other times not. Once I worked with a woman for three hours before she touched her center. That was unusually long.

Often, people incorrectly think that a *longing* for something is an energy of the heart. Longing is not an energy. Longing is, in fact, a direct signal, of the energy that already exists. It signals you already possess at your heart what you long for. Actually, what you long for is to *function* in a way that matches the energy of the heart. For example, if you say, "I really long to be a friend of that person," then, already in your heart, you love. Your longing is to actualize in your behavior what you already possess. Joelyn was already a carefree woman who longed to express it in her behavior. Our longing feelings relate to *doing* that which we already are in our *being*.

Next, I want to caution you to stay away from the *objects* of you energies. As I indicated in the first example, I felt nurturing toward *myself*. But as I enter more deeply into my center I try to dissociate from the object of the nurturing. The object will come later, out there. I do not want to focus on "out there." Consequently, I try to let go of the objects my energies are directed toward while at the bottom of my U.

Finally, if you feel stuck in the process you can try looking for the "flip side" of what you are caught in. At times, you will become mired in negative and uncomfortable feelings. It will seem like you cannot get through a particular layer. Worry, fear, sadness or upset are the kinds of layers I mean. When that happens, it might be helpful for you to look for the flip side of that feeling.

The flip side is that feeling or experience that tends to go along with whatever it is that makes you feel stuck. You have flip sides to all your experiences. For example, if you enter yourself and sense shyness you may not like it, and gradually get stuck in it. It is then helpful to ask: "What goes along with my being shy? What other characteristic or quality do I tend also to show?" The answer may be gentleness. If you are shy, you are probably also fairly gentle. Then you focus on your gentleness, and you have moved out of the stuck spot.

A few other instances will help clarify this. If you are caught up in anger, what goes along with that? If there is anger, there is usually passion. And I do not mean sexual passion. I simply mean passion for living. Then go with passion for living.

Perhaps you are stuck in sadness from a significant

loss of a friend. You could only feel such loss if you have loved deeply. Now you can focus on your loving energy rather than the loss of your friend. Maybe you have been trapped in stubborness. Convictedness goes with stubborness. Focus then on your faithful conviction and your single-heartedness. In these ways, then, you can help yourself out of the traps in the process to your heart.

In a geographical journey it is most helpful to know your destination before you begin. In psychological journeys, knowing the finish line too soon can inhibit the process and make the discovery less complete. Consequently, I have not shared with you what you can expect to find at your heart in any detail. Let me conclude this chapter by stating the four basic energies you will find at your heart.

The first energy is to *exist*. We move toward existence at all times. Not only do we drive for physical existence, but also for psychological and interpersonal existence as well. This energy shows itself dramatically when we are ignored by other people or rejected by others.

The second energy is the *exist as best as we possibly can*. We all want to be whole and to live as rich and as satisfying lives as possible. Part of our nature is to live up to our nature as completely as possible. Part of this energy shows itself in our movement toward happiness, contentment and peacefulness.

The third energy is that of *freedom*. We strive to function independently and to be self-determining people. We want to take charge of our own lives and destinies. We seek choices and alternative ways of acting and reacting.

Finally, the fourth energy is that of *love*. This, perhaps, flows as the most humanizing energy we have. Two sides appear to that energy. We move toward caring for others; and we move toward belonging to others. Sometimes we experience one dimension of this energy more than the other. At a particular time we may move toward others to serve and care for them. And at other times, we may need to be cared for and loved. Both those elements come from the energy of love within us. All of us possess these four energies. In different circumstances and at different times, one energy may be stronger than another. And each energy is filled with rich nuances that we discover in our efforts to touch our inner lives. It is in touching those various and surprising shades of these four basic energies that we will discover our own goodness is fresh and invigorating ways.

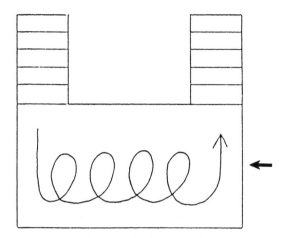

11: FROM THE HEART INTO ACTION

We have started this process on the outside of ourselves in our feelings and behaviors. We have journeyed inward and downward to hear the voice of our heart and to reach our core energies so that we can live faithfully to our truest self. Once we reach those energies we need to give them power so they can rise up the other side of the U and surface in functions that match our heart.

Our first task, then, after we have identified our core energies, is to empower them. We do that by focusing on those energies. Remember the basic psychological principle: We give power to what we focus on. Once we know the energy, we focus on it, attempting to let it grow within us, so that it begins to fill us and propel us to act directly out of that energy.

How can you help those energies to grow? One way I find very helpful for myself and others is this: Try to picture that energy as a small dot of light in the middle of your body. The inside of your body is dark and hollow, with this tiny speck of light. Keep focused on the light and gradually expand it so that it soon fills the entire cavern of your body.

For example, if I feel the nurturing energy discussed earlier and want to expand it, then I imagine it as a small dot of light gradually filling me up. I give that light a small voice of its own and let it speak to me. It says: "I am your energy. I am your nurturing." The voice and the light become louder and brighter so that I actually feel the energy in my body. And that is who I am, a nurturing loving person. No longer am I focused on my tiredness or frustration. I am centered on my nurturing. I give it power by focusing on it.

As this energy fills us up, we become ready to let it rise up to the other side of the U, back into the outer world and into our behavior and feelings. Basically, this energy will surface in two ways: the first is by explosion of the energies through the inhibiting layer; and second, by our ability to pull out those layers that sabotage the energies from coming up directly.

In the explosion method, we so focus on the energy of our hearts, that we can literally no longer contain that power. It bursts through no matter what layers of past experience or what beliefs we have to retain that energy.

For instance, I am in a group and I have some important things to say, but I am too shy to say them. That feeling and behavior of shyness comes from a rich and good energy within me. But that energy has gotten tangled up with layers in me such as "If I say anything, people will think I am dumb." So my energy of freedom comes up, hits that layer and surfaces in shy behavior. Well, if I focus intently on my freedom energy and give it power, then it may grow strong enough in me to shoot right through that inhibiting layer about my being dumb if I speak. By focusing on my freedom I can say to myself: "I don't give a darn what other people think about this. I need to be free to say what is important to me." And I speak. I have, then, been faithful to the voice of my heart rather than to old outside voices.

Another example: The energy in me is love. It is directed to a certain person. But when I see that person I do not go out to him, because I am afraid of his response. Now, once again, if I so focus on the energy of loving within me, then that energy of love can literally explode through the layer that says: "Maybe he won't like what I'm doing, or maybe he will misunderstand me, and reject me; and that would be terrible." If I explode that layer by focusing on my love, then my loving will rise up directly and express itself in a way that matches with my heart.

The key to the explosion process is to stay very open to the energies of your heart, and to keep yourself focused on those energies so they will rise up more fully in you and find direct expression in feelings and behaviors that match the energies of your heart. The result is personal harmony and inner peace.

The second approach to letting our energies surface involves our ability to identify and pull out all inhibiting layers. Then our energies will rise up in us in direct ways. These layers, as discussed throughout this book, are made up of beliefs and attitudes learned during our lives. Unfortunately, we believe them all, even though many are not true. It is these faulty beliefs that tend to serve as inhibiting layers. In order to yank out these layers we need a healthy distrust of our beliefs. It helps us to be willing to challenge our beliefs. They are not true just because we believe them. If we can be open to challenging our layers, then we have a good chance of breaking down those that inhibit our energies from flowing directly to the top of us (our functioning).

Dramatic beliefs cause us a lot of trouble. As discussed in the chapter on anxiety, dramatic layers accelerate the intensity of our feelings, which, in turn, has the effect of forcing us to act in habitual, oftentimes, non-helping ways. If we pay attention to our layers and notice dramatic thoughts, we help ourselves by challenging those and attempting to de-dramatize them. Interpersonally, for instance, we can dramatize the possibility of rejection. Consequently, we may not even go out toward another person we like. By identifying the dramatic layer, we can then challenge the possibility of rejection, and, perhaps, pull out that layer, allowing our loving energy to show itself in warm and responsive behavior.

A second set of layers that can sabotage our energies is *demands*. Demand layers tend to take our energies of love and freedom and turn them into angry actions. Demand thoughts are made up of all the shoulds and musts that we use to regulate everybody's life. Let's say I really love you, but when you treated me that awful way, I felt hurt and anger at the top of me, and love at the core of me. I am hurt and angry precisely because I love you. So up comes my loving energy, but hits a demand layer that says: "You should never do such a thing to me." That entangles my love and out comes anger.

As you go through the U process, especially the more structured way, notice any demand layers. Send up red flags when you hit them, telling yourself you need to challenge those. Try to pull the demands out, and replace them with wishes. And try to accept reality as it is rather than how you insist it must be.

Keep in mind the goal of all this: we are trying to get in touch with our inner energies so we know who we are; and then we want to try getting our top layer (our feelings and behaviors) to match up with those energies in direct and clear ways. In that match up we will find inner peace.

In order to check how well your top layer of functioning matches up with the energies of your heart, you might want to keep a simple diary. In that diary you try to record your daily events. You simply identify each behavioral setting you enter. You indicate who is in the setting. You write down briefly what you were feeling and what you were doing. And then you try to identify the energy of your heart at that moment. Finally, you record if your feelings and behaviors matched the energy of your heart or not.

So, for example, a recording might look like this:

"Kitchen: Joelyn, Andy, and Amy present. All of us are eating breakfast. Feeling relaxed. Energy: to live fully. Match: Yes."

"Staff meeting. Whole staff there. Feeling impatient; talking with some irritation. Energy: to be free. Match:

No."

Doing this recording will make you very aware of how well your functions match your heart. In those situations, where your heart and functions did not match, you can then ask yourself how you could have functioned differently. That way, you continue teaching yourself to create behaviors that match your inner energies. Certainly, the more aware of your energies you become, the more likely you will look for functions to match those energies.

The practicality of this kind of reflection cannot be overstated. Occasions of conflict are some of the best times for reflection on the match between our behavior and our energies. Most frequently people in conflict do not match their heart with their behavior. Often people who are in conflict with one another feel bonded to each other at some other level.

In marriage, for example, the two people may care for each other, but find themselves using argumentative stances toward one another. They yell, shout, use obscenities, or remain silent and pout. That is their behavior; but what do they find in their hearts? Most likely, they would discover a desire to feel valued and loved by the other, to be happy and at one with their spouse. But what comes out is their anger and hostility.

If they could pause for a moment and ask themselves: "What is in my heart? What do I truly seek?" the answers they discover would alter the dynamic of conflict. They would probably discover a feeling of hurt; and under that, they might discover a desire to be in a loving relationship with their spouse. So, love moves in their heart and anger flows out of them toward their partners. Of course, there is no match. In fact, their behavior (anger) drives a deeper wedge in the relationship they both desire.

Recognizing the mismatch, they might ask themselves: "If I were to speak and act directly out of my heart, what might I say and do?" The wife might say: "Look, Tom, I guess I'm upset with you because I love you. I know that sounds crazy, but I so want our relationship to be good for both of us, that sometimes I end up yelling to get it that way. I just want us to be close. I want to be friends."

While this approach may not solve every conflict all by itself, it reframes the conflict in an atmosphere of caring rather than attack. Someone once suggested that "confrontation" is handled better when it is done in a "care-fronting" manner. When we express what lies in our hearts we will feel whole and integral.

Let me show you, practically, how I try to bring the energies of my heart to the surface. As I indicated earlier, each morning I try to gain a sense of who I am, what energies appear to be moving within me. If I recognize I am a nurturer, then throughout that day I try to reinforce that energy and act out of it directly. Today I must see nine clients in therapy. I can look at that schedule at 8:00 A.M. and say: "Oh my heavens, one person after another without any break." If I stay focused on nine people without a break, I will become exhausted by the third person. I will continue all day hoping to finish this giant task.

Or I can focus on my inner energy as a nurturer. Today I am a nurturing and caring person. How can I nurture this person I see at 8:00 A.M.? Between each appointment, I take 30 seconds and again refresh myself with the awareness that I am a nurturer, and want to act according to that energy. By doing this I find I become less tired and much more attentive to the person I am working with, whether that person comes at 8:00 A.M. or 4:00 P.M.

Sometimes the energy of caring will be directed toward ourselves. By focusing on his core, one man realized that part of his caring had to be done *to himself.* He was so busy at work responding to others, he rarely took time to go to the bathroom. (Now, that's a tight schedule.) The expression of his caring energy surfaced in a commitment to go to the bathroom no matter how far behind he was in his schedule. He discovered a reduction in impatience and a greater attentiveness to details in his work.

Perhaps, most significantly, my reaction to my children seems more loving when I am aware of who I am at my heart. The other day, in my den with my door closed, I realized I was a provider. Shortly afterward, my young daughter opened the door and came in. I had ten tasks to do at my desk. Had I not been aware that I am a loving provider and that I can best provide for my children with my presence, I am sure I would have told Amy I had much to do and she should go and watch cartoons on T.V. But instead I set my pen down and invited her in. She sat on my lap for two minutes and we talked and hugged. When she left, I felt whole, and I returned to my ten tasks.

Summary

The major steps in the U process of discovering our energies and acting out of them are as follows:
1) We learn to attend to our outside voices and to our inside voice.
2) We learn to separate and distinguish those two voices.
3) We attempt to form our identity based on our inside voice rather than on the outside voices.
4) We realize that our feelings and behaviors operate at the outer edge of our life, and do not constitute our identity.
5) We realize that our feelings and behaviors serve as direct or indirect signals of our inner energies.
6) We attempt to discover our core energies by *entering* our feelings, behaviors and all the layers of our life. We do not reject or deny any voice that speaks within us, but *enter* whatever lies there. We enter either by going through each and every layer in a structured way; or we enter in a less structured, more feeling manner.

7) Once we reach our center and discover our energies, we give them power by focusing on them.
8) By focusing on our energies, we expand them. Then we can embrace them and affirm them as who we are.
9) Finally, we try to allow those energies to rise up in us and surface in matching feelings and behavior. This can happen by the explosion process of challenging and extracting the sabotaging layers.

By following this process, we will experience a fuller sense of integrity and wholeness. We live the human life when our outer functions match well with our inner being. We then reveal the beauty and richness of human nature. Our work as people, then, is to get our heart's energies to surface in feelings and behavior that match and express the movements of love and freedom, which fully determine our humanity.

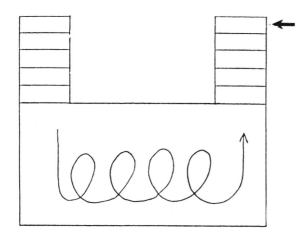

12: FROM THE HEART INTO RELATIONSHIPS

Having listened to and affirmed the voices of our heart, we will experience those deep energies within us rising up in behaviors of love and freedom. Translated into specific behavioral skills, the energy of love shows itself in our ability to form significant *relationships* with others; and the energy of freedom reveals itself in making choices to engage the flow of our life rather than deny it.

We turn first to the skill of building and maintaining personal relationships.

Embedded within the very core of our nature dwells a force that continually moves us toward other people in loving ways. We may not always act according to that energy, but it remains constant and alive in us. Recall Gabriel Marcel's claim that our first awareness is "We are, therefore I am."

Given the energy in us to bond with other people in caring relationships, we need to develop bonding skills. Two particular skills lead to bonding with others: the skill of receiving another person and the skill of self-revelation.

Receiving Another

The foundation for receiving another person lies in our ability and desire to be open to people. If we have formed our judgments about people before we come to know them, bonding will not easily occur, especially if our judgments flash negatively. Prejudice, racism, agism, sexism happen because we have judged persons without all the data. The result is disconnectedness.

When my son entered second grade we had heard negative comments about his teacher. My wife and I were set not to like her and to do battle with her for the education of our son. Andy had not heard the negative comments, so he went to second grade in a receiving and open stance. As the school year went on we were amazed at how much he liked his teacher and how well he was doing in school. He had bonded well with her because he was set to receive her from the beginning.

In order to receive someone well, we help ourselves by *slowing down* our internal responses to that person. Often, we race around inside our minds looking for something vital to say, or wc hear ourselves disagreeing before the person has freely stated his/her belief. Our quick response or interruption of someone are signs we are going too fast inside. Instead of "knowing what they will say before they say it," can we lay back, take a deep breath and let them take us through the many trails of their minds until they reach the real message they have for us?

When somebody begins talking with me, I try to think of his or her mind as a maze. At the center of the maze lies the real message attempting to be communicated. When the person — let's call him John — opens his mouth and speaks to me, we then stand together at the "starting point" of his mind's maze.

My job, as *receiver*, is to let him take me through that maze, hitting dead ends and circling around the outer edges, until he comes into the center. I cannot assume that the first words out of his mouth express accurately and fully the message at the core. Most of us are not that much in touch with our deepest self to state clearly on the first try what moves deeply within us. So, if I simply stay with John, tracking around through his mind he has a better chance of reaching his center and I have greater odds of bonding well to him.

We see the need to slow down most dramatically in relating to children. Because oftentimes they do not know the center of their maze, they circle around the edges for longer periods of time. Frequently, they will begin a conversation on one issue, but really be heading for deeper issues.

Fifteen year old Anne might begin talking about how "neat" it would be to have a steady boyfriend. If her parents take her statement as the full expression of her mind and heart, they might jump all over her. End of discussion. On the other hand, if the parents slow down and realize Anne's statement only allows them to enter her maze, then the journey can begin. As they stay with Ann, simply receiving her they may discover she is much more concerned about getting along with her girl friends at school than she is about going steady. Greater bonding results when she feels understood because her parents tracked through her maze to the goal at the center.

Closely linked to slowing down internally is the need to stay out of our world while receiving another. Setting aside, temporarily, our own beliefs, feelings, values, experiences and attitudes may not seem easy to do, but it is critical in our effort to bond to another person. Just because we follow someone else's thoughts and feeling, does not mean we agree. Agreeing and understanding operate in very different ways.

When we stay away from our views momentarily, and attend to the other, we say, in effect, "I respect and value you, and so want to know how you view things. I may then agree or disagree." The spirit of receiving someone translates to a deep desire to *know* that person. I want to get inside that individual and see how he/she thinks and values and judges because however they view life, it can enrich my own life.

One of the difficulties in letting go of our own world and staying in another's has to do with the amount of information we need to live in this world. Whenever we make a choice to respond to a person or situation, we need a certain amount of data. If we do not have enough hard information, we tend to supply what is missing from our own personal view and experience. When people talk to us, they usually do not offer us one hundred percent of the available information. They leave blank spaces in their sentences. Our tendency is to fill in those blanks from *our own* experience. Sometimes we may guess right and sometimes not.

When we fill in the missing blanks in another's message to us, we add *interpretation* to *information*. The communication principle is: The more information a person has, the less interpretation he/she will do; the less information, the more interpretation will occur.

Data Needed

INFORMATION	INTERPRETATION	INFORMATION	INTERPRETATION

Our interpretations arise primarily from within ourselves rather than from the outside world. To interpret, we mix some sensory data, some stereotypic beliefs, some emotions, some guesses, some self-concept and some values. If our interpretations fit what the other person left unsaid, we will bond well to that individual. If the interpretations do not fit that person's reality, misunderstanding will result.

I hear a business associate say: "I really don't like making those phone calls to clients." If I do not seek more information I will then add my interpretations as to the meaning of his statement. I may fill in the missing blanks with: "Then, he will not make those calls." I respond to my interpretation and become angry with him for not doing his job.

Perhaps, had I stayed out of my world of interpretations and slowed them down, I might have gathered additional information from him. By staying with him in his world I might have understood how fearful he is in making these phone calls. Knowing he must make the calls tomorrow begins causing anxiety today. He still intends on making the calls, but cannot get himself to like doing it.

Now my interpretation and response might be considerably different. Instead of anger he may receive my compassion and support. And we more likely remain bonded.

Strong and oftentimes inaccurate interpretations occur because we remain locked in our own world view and do not walk with the other long enough. To take the stance of seeking more and more information from another allows us to stand right up alongside that person letting him or her know we are there.

Finally, to receive others well, it helps to let them know that you did receive them and track with them through their minds and hearts. I am most amazed by our ability to recognize the feelings of others even if they do not state those feelings directly. In marriage counselling, I will often ask the husband if he can notice how his wife feels. He will say, "hurt" or "sad" or "angry." And nine times out of ten he will be on target. However, he never let her know he knew how she felt.

We oftentimes receive others very well, but do not let them know we have gotten the message. When we do let them know we understand — by telling them *what* we understand — it completes the bonding process. They have shared; we have received and let them know what we received. If our receiving was accurate, the givers will feel connected or bonded to us. They will feel accepted because they have been understood.

Many books, lectures and workshops on communication highlight this important step of feeding back what we have received. They teach us to say: "It sounds like you are very sad;" or "I hear you saying...;" or "So, you think grandma should come for the holidays."

These phrases can make our conversation feel stilted and inauthentic. It does not feel natural. A man reported to me, after taking a five day seminar on communication, that "this feedback stuff is really dumb." He reached this conclusion when he arrived home from the seminar. His wife met him at the door, greeted him warmly with a hug and kiss, and said excitedly: "I'm so happy you're home. I missed you so much." He responded, practicing his new-found feedback skill: "So, you're really glad to see me." After she withdrew from his arms and stared questioningly at him, he said he would never do "reflective listening" again. It just did not fit.

While the *techniques* of feedback may feel stiff and unnatural at the beginning, the *spirit* of feedback needs to be present in any communication process. That spirit involves our ability to let the other person know we have received and understood. If our desire is to stand with the other's unique experience of the world, then we will naturally tend to let that person know we have received his or her message. With all our faculties focused on the other person we will spontaneously check with him or her periodically to make sure we are tracking accurately. We might say: "Wait a second. Let me see if I understand what you're saying..." And then tell them what we heard. Or we might ask a clarifying question like: "Now, are you saying you should or shouldn't take out that loan for your business?"

Teachers give tests to students to see if the students received the information. It is not sufficient for the teacher to ask at the end of a course: "Did you all understand the material this semester?" And when the students say "yes," the teacher gives them all A's. In the same way, the giver needs the receiver to tell what has been received. It is not sufficient to simply state: "Ah,

yes, I understand." Telling the other *what* we understand
lets him or her know we walk with them through the
maze. Such understanding bonds people heart to heart.

Self-Revelation

The other side of bonding involves the sharing of
ourselves with others. Self-revelation does not come
easily for many people. They may not know themselves
well enough to reveal much personally. They may be
afraid of standing exposed to another. They may believe
that others will dislike them if they reveal their true
selves ("If you really knew me, you wouldn't like me.")
So, for a variety of reasons, some people will not share
their inner selves. To the degree that they fail to do so,
they will not feel bonded to others.

To become self-revealing, we need to believe that
the less we mask, the more others will like us. Usually,
the people we dislike are those who mask their real self.
They play roles, such as the know-it-all, the authority
figure, the queen-bee, the goody-two-shoes, etc. When
we try to fake it, we will lose connectedness.

On the other hand, when we take down the masks
and show our true self with all our strengths and
weaknesses, we find ourselves more receivable by
others and more acceptable.

To this day when I give talks or workshops to young
children I seem to to better when I stumble over words or
misspell a word on the blackboard. They shout and howl,
but seem more bonded to me. It teaches me that bonding
has little to do with our perfection; it has to do with our
sincerity and integrity. To show limitation along with
strength lets others know we need them.

In marriage counseling, I will quite frequently hear
a husband or a wife complain that their spouse no longer
needs them for anything. That sense causes a couple to
drift apart. Strange as it seems, people move toward each
other the more they recognize one another's needs. If my
wife is always strong and "got it all together" then my

practical ways of loving her get reduced. Her need as well as her strength attracts me and bonds us more deeply.

The spirit of self-revelation lies in our desire to let others know the real us. When I want to bond with someone I try hard to share spontaneously whatever I sense within me, believing that the process of honesty and openness is what the other finds attractive, rather than the content of my words. Most of us have lived enough life to accept the limitations and deficiencies in other people. What we value and cherish is the free sharing and open expression of who we are.

To act in self-revealing ways, we need to live close to our heart. If we know the energies that move deeply within us, we will find the words to say in every situation. Speaking of what lies at the core of us will make us transparent and available to others.

How profoundly I know this truth. When I first met and fell in love with my wife, I spoke to her from my heart, telling her of my love for her. But after a while we decided to end our relationship for work related and geographical reasons. For the next four years, we remained separated. Throughout that time, the whisper of my heart said I still loved her like I never loved anyone before. But I thought she might have other life goals and relationships that would not include me. So I kept the quiet voice within me muted. I did not heed it. So I did not act on it.

But the voice of love kept on whispering my feelings for Joelyn. Finally, four years later, I could not restrain that constant sound. I attended to my heart's energy. I went to Chicago, found Joelyn and revealed to her my feelings. I told her I still loved her and wanted to see if we could build our relationship again. To my delight, she told me her love for me still burned brightly, and, yes, she would want to explore again the relationship we once had.

My only regret in this story is the lack of attention I paid to my heart those four years. Had I listened sooner I might have revealed my continued love for Joelyn after one year instead of four. This life-giving relationship started much later than it needed, because I failed to listen to my heart.

Resolving Conflicted Relationships

In most relationships people will eventually experience conflict. It may occur because of a misunderstanding, or a difference of opinion, or someone being ignored. It may develop into a large complex conflict or remain a simple, slightly annoying difference. But, nonetheless, if we form interpersonal relationships we can expect conflict.

Generally, conflict arises around the issue of *needs*. When David looks to Sharon to satisfy his need for companionship, and she fails to do so, conflict will begin to develop. When one nation "needs" the land occupied by another nation, conflict, called war, results.

In interpersonal relationships, *mutual* need satisfaction forms the basis of continued contact. Certainly, we see this in business arrangements. Presently, we are building a sun room onto our house. I needed a general contractor to take care of this project for me. He needed me to pay him so that he earns an income. As soon as the addition is completed and the bills paid, we will no longer need each other and the relationship will end.

While this analysis may appear somewhat stark and hard, I think you will notice the same dynamic in friendships as well as business contacts. We have all had close friendships that gradually or abruptly died away. Why? Fundamentally because we no longer *needed* each other. I remember my grade school friends. We needed each other to play basketball. We needed each other for "hanging around" purposes. When high school came, I played sports with other friends, and "hung around" with them also. I no longer needed my earlier friends, nor they me. So we went our own ways. Today, my friends need me and I need them — for companionship, for someone to talk to, for a playmate, for shopping expeditions, for heart-to-heart sharings.

Even marriages succeed or fail based on the satisfaction of both partner's needs. If a couple's needs are fulfilled by each other the relationship endures. Some people hold the notion that married love can be altruistic. When a couple marries they promise to love each other "for better or for worse, for richer or for poorer, in sickness and in health until death do us part." That sounds quite altruistic. However, a rather profound *condition* lies under this beautiful promise: "I will love you this way as long as you love me this way." The bond in marriage, friendship or almost any relationship is modified by the condition of *mutual need fulfillment.* As a marriage counselor, I do not see marriages last when one or both parties fail to satisfy the human needs of the other.

Perhaps the relationship of a parent to a child comes closest to altruistic love. Although most parents' need for nurturing and procreating may be met in parenting, the same mutuality found in adult friendships does not exist with children. Parents often love their children without any expectation of return. Often parents do not look to their children to satisfy their needs; they simply love the children for their own sake.

I hope the point is clear: Needs and the lack of their satisfaction lie as the basic cause of conflict in interpersonal relationships.

At least four inter-related elements occur around need fulfillment in a relationship:

1. Awareness of needs. An individual might be aware of his/her need or might not be that consciously in touch with the need.
2. Expression of needs. A person may express the need directly, indirectly, or not at all.
3. Response to needs. The other person may choose to minister to the need or decide not to minister it.
4. Results. If the need is expressed and satisfied

by the other, the result is gratitude and a continuation of the relationship. if the need is not fulfilled, conflict arises.

A number of patterns occur.

First, Peter was married to Julie for eight years. He had a strong need for intimacy with his wife, but remained unaware of that need. He knew something was amiss, but could not label it. Although sex had always been pleasurable for him, he felt vaguely unfulfilled by it. He could not express his need to his wife because he was unaware of it. She could not respond because she did not know what was the matter.

Julie sensed something happening to Peter, but felt helpless in responding to it. Peter began feeling restless and vaguely dissatisfied with his life and with his wife.

Second, Sandy comes home from a long day at work, expecting her room-mate, Barbara, to have the meal ready. Monday is Barbara's night for cooking. Sandy finds a bland, T.V. dinner set before her. She is aware of her need for a good home-cooked meal, but does not express her need to Barbara. Many reasons may exist to explain why Sandy does not express her need. She may fear Barbara's angry response; she may believe she should not have any needs; she might think Barbara will be hurt; she does not want to sound like a nagging room-mate, and so on.

Without the direct expression of her need, Sandy will probably try to express it indirectly. She might sulk during the meal; leave most of her food on the plate; or bang cupboard doors while cleaning up afterward. She will gradually become resentful toward Barbara for not knowing and responding to her needs. She says to herself: "We've lived together for three years. By this time you should know what I need without me asking for it every day." In a word, Sandy becomes passive aggressive.

Third, Donna had been aware of her need to be number one priority in Kevin's life. She has repeatedly expressed that need to him over the 17 years of their marriage. Sports has dominated his life all this time. He coaches high school basketball and track, referees football games, and plays on three softball teams in the summer.

When her need for special attention was not met over the years, she would ask for it in stronger and more repetitious ways. It got to be nagging. Then she became resentful, followed by hurt and discouragement. Finally, she withdrew from him, and sought a divorce.

Fourth, Fred wants Alice to help trim the grass. He knows his need and expresses it directly. Alice responds, but in *parity*. She will help him only if he picks up the prescription at the druggist. This leads to scorekeeping, which sets up the rhythm for an antagonistic, contestual relationship.

Needs	Expressed	Response From Others
1. Unaware	Not directly	No response
2. Aware	Not directly	No response
3. Aware	Directly	No response
4. Aware	Directly	In parity

We avoid conflict by being aware of our needs, expressing them directly, and hoping the other person ministers to those needs.

Dynamics of Conflict

Polarization

When a difference arises between people, they attempt to convince each other of the correctness of their position. To do so, they highlight just how different one position is from the other. Each person will also dramatize his or her view to demonstrate how right he or she is.

Two business partners decide to paint their store. Shiela wants green and Rose wants blue. They decide to look at blue-green colors. At the paint store Shiela finds a color shade slightly more green than blue. Rose does not like it and says: "That's too light. It's almost all green."

Shiela says, "It's got more blue in it than green." And the two begin creating the great chasm.

Rose says: "That's such a light green, it's almost yellow."

Shiela counters: "It's so blue, it looks like navy blue."

Eventually, Rose has the color pure white, and Shiela presents it as pitch black. They have carried the argument to its extremes, in order to convince each other how right they are. Significantly, as they distort the reality in order to persuade the other, they gradually begin to believe the distortion. Of course, their own position, then, looks even more correct, and the other person's view becomes obviously more ridiculous.

Part of the polarizing process includes making irrational and not-sensical the other's position. "*All* you *ever* want to do," says the upset wife, "is have sex. It's your answer to *everything*." The husband counters: "In your eyes, *all* I'm worth around here is my pay check." By making the other person's position absurd, we think we strengthen our own.

Personalize

Once we have polarized our positions, we tend to turn the argument into a personal issue. Once Shiela and Rose push the substantive issue (the color of the paint) to its limits, and have nowhere else to go with it, they turn it into a personal attack.

Rose says: "Shiela, you're so color-blind you couldn't tell white from black even if it was spelled out before you."

Shiela shouts back: "And you're so stubborn, no wonder you never got married. No man would want you."

Soon the issue of the wall color is lost, and the two are attacking one another. This attacking creates stronger defenses and closed attitudes in both parties, making it even more difficult to resolve the conflict.

Other Perceived as Enemy

When two people conflict, they usually perceive the other as "against them." They also tend to blame the other for the problem. In marriage counselling, I regularly see the husband blame the wife for the difficulties ("If she would just quit nagging and accept me as I am..."), and the wife blame the husband (If he would only spend a little time with me..."). We maintain and intensify conflict by perceiving the other as the "villain."

When the other is "wrong" or "bad," then naturally, I am "correct" or "right." The relationship now takes on a contest-like atmosphere. I try to win; I try to make the other lose. We no longer cooperate with each other. Instead, we pull against the other, oftentimes in an antagonistic manner.

With the winner-loser spirit inherent in conflict, the players take on offensive and defensive roles. Offensively, many people use anger to win the game. Defensively, people usually feel hurt, thus building up walls to protect themselves. (You might want to return to Chapter 6 on anger to review the interaction of anger and hurt.) Anger tends to break down the fabric of a relationship. It can keep the antagonistic feelings high. Hurt also breaks down the bonding between people, as it leads to a protective response that excludes the other.

Demands

When our needs are not met in a relationship, they will often turn into demands. What begins as hopes and wishes gradually changes into emphatic commands. "You must be on time!" "You should call every night." "You can't leave me now!" "You have to be more sensitive to my needs."

Demands serve as a strong statement of need. Of course, when someone makes a demand of us, we will tend to resist it. We follow the interpersonal principle: The greater the force exerted against us, the greater will be our resistance. Thus, demands generally do not work well in the satisfaction of our needs. Eventually, the demands, if they remain unmet, turn into angry accusations that undercut the bonds of the relationship. Furthermore, the anger and harshness obscure the expression of need underneath. We end up dealing with the anger and hurt, rather than the needs we have of each other.

Responding To Conflict

To reduce conflicts and keep them from ruining a relationship, active steps and attitudes can be taken. Each of these responses can help keep conflicts from expanding to the point of hurt and serious alienation.

De-dramatize the positions

Since polarizing positions distort the issue being contested, staying close to the facts keeps us within the range of reality. Try not to dramatize your position in order to influence the other. Saying such things as "I've told you a million times..." is not true, and begins the twisted cycle of misunderstanding and hostility. Better to say, "I've told you a number of times..." or "I've told you often in the past weeks..."

"Always" or "never" are the kind of words that dramatize our position. "You *always* come late to work." "You *never* consider my feelings." "You are *forever* complaining about my other friends." These statements need to give way to less powerful expressions.

First of all, it works better to talk about ourselves rather than the other person. Saying, "I need you to be more sensitive to my feelings," works better than accusing, "You never pay attention to me."

Secondly, we take out all the emotionally packed words. We will keep the conflict small by using small-powered words, like "occasionally," "it seems like," "once in a while," "I wish," rather than the universal words that allow no exceptions.

Stay Away From Personal Attacks

The waters of conflict muddy considerably when we begin attacking the person rather than the issue. Try to stay with the issue instead of the emotional reaction to the person. This can be difficult, because we often take personally people's differences with us. We need to maintain as much objectivity in the conflict as possible. If we hear ourselves resorting to name-calling or ridicule, we know objectivity is lost.

At times, we might even attack the vulnerable spots of our friend. We get caught up in the fight and say things we normally guard against in saner moments. If I know my friend gets caught by guilt, I might try to induce that in the argument. If my wife is sensitive to her weight, then I use that in the midst of the conflict.

Before any conflict occurs, it is helpful to commit yourself to never attacking the person at those vulnerable positions they have shared in moments of trust. What our friend offers at these awesome times needs to be guarded by us as a sacred responsibility.

Use GRIT

In the late fifties, Charles Osgood, a social psychologist, developed a process to reduce international conflict, called "The Gradual Reduction in Tension," or GRIT. Although the theory appeared sound, it did not work out well in practice for a variety of reasons.

However, what did not work in the international arena has had better success at the interpersonal level.

Osgood pointed out how we perceive other persons in conflict as the enemy. To break the conflict, he said, we need to help the other persons change their perception of us as their enemy to a view of us as a friend. This could be accomplished by unilateral gestures and actions of friendship toward the people who see us as "the bad guy." To change the other's perception will take perseverance and consistency. We must demonstrate through our actions that we are *with* the person, and not *against* him or her. We cannot look for any return of kindness for a while. The other person will doubt the sincerity of our good will gestures at first, and so, will remain defensive. Gradually, having experienced our regular cooperative efforts, that person will most likely begin to reciprocate kindness for kindness.

I saw this process work most dramatically six years ago in marriage counselling. The couple was so antagonistic they could not talk with each other in my office at the same time. So I split the sessions — first seeing one, then the other. I decided to try GRIT. I explained the process to the husband and asked what he could do to show his wife he was on her side. He could think of nothing (which was part of the problem). I learned he packed his own lunch in the morning, much to his chagrin, and went off to work without saying anything to his wife. I commented: "Tomorrow morning you say to her 'Goodbye, I hope you have a nice day.'"

The following week the couple returned. I asked the wife: "How did the week go?" She said: "Dr. Olen, whatever you told him last week worked wonders. He seemed warmer toward me somehow." She could not identify what he did differently, but just sensed he was not so much her enemy.

I then saw the husband and asked him how the week went. He responded: "Dr. Olen, I don't know what you told her last week, but it sure helped." I had told her nothing. Because he showed her some little sign of friendship each morning, she responded at a less than conscious level, more as a friend as well.

We were on a roll. I asked if he could think of anything else he could now do. Again, nothing came to mind. I suggested: "When you arrive home in the evening, you say to her: 'Hi. How was your day?' And then you wait while she tells you." He followed my instructions, again with the same results. His wife felt better about him, and he felt better about her. Soon after that we were able to continue marriage counselling all together.

Developing Interior Beliefs

Certain attitudes and beliefs help us respond to conflict in productive ways. These beliefs predispose us to keep conflicts small and managable.

First of all, it helps to realize that a contest can take place only if two people play in it. You cannot have a winner and a loser it only one person enters the contest. Remaining focused on making the other person and me both winners will keep me in a cooperative stance. If I work to create winners, the antagonistic dynamic never gets started. By getting caught up in the winner-loser process, I only reinforce the game-like style of the other person. And the conflict will tend to remain in place and eventually accelerate.

My own favorite belief in reducing conflict and much tension in life is: *In the great scheme of life's events, very little is important.* This belief has helped me to keep much of reality in perspective and to hold conflict to a minimum. Fortunately, I married a woman who holds the same belief. So, when we have a difference of views, that issue remains small. It does not, then, touch our friendship. Furthermore, it fades quickly as we see it in an even larger perspective. As a friend commented to me recently: "Many of our problems and conflicts are about as big as whether these older chairs go with this newer rug." I continue to be amused that the "big problems" of our lives often become the most interesting and humorous stories we tell two months later.

Having a sense of humor also helps keep conflict in perspective. Just as there is negative in every positive, so is there positive in every negative. Humor lies within the serious, just as seriousness can be found in most humor. So, it helps to look for the light side, to enjoy the moment of delight in the struggle. To do so, it helps to see the humorous element early in the conflict. Once the struggle becomes too intense, the humor often turns to sarcasm.

Finally, a belief needing work in most of us is: *When there are two opposing views, both are valid, only different.* I discussed this belief in Chapter 6. I bring it back here because it applies so well to conflict. If I keep accepting as valid for him or her the other person's view, I will not tend toward anger. And, if I also accept my view as valid for me, I will avoid hurt and defensiveness. Without anger, hurt, and defensiveness to interfere, I and my friend have a good chance of resolving our differences, before the conflict turns destructive.

Separate Self from the Other

In interpersonal conflict, we easily give creative power to the other person. To avoid this, it helps to keep in mind a profound belief stated in the first book of the scriptures. From the beginning, the writers make it clear that God's word is creative. "God said, 'Let there be light,' and so it was. God said, 'Let there be birds in the air and fishes in the sea,' and so it was." In other words, when God spoke, things happened.

But the same is not necessarily true for us humans. Just because someone calls me a jerk during an argument, does not make me a jerk. Their words have no bearing on the reality. I was either a jerk or not a jerk independently of the other's statement.

People only have creative power in our life when we

give them that power. To avoid giving them such power, it helps to realize that *whatever the other person says is a statement about him or her, and not a statement about us.* Even when the person is expressing strong feelings about us, he or she is really telling us something about him or herself.

A man and woman are riding home from a party. She has been upset with his behavior all night, and lets him have it in the car. She barks: "You act like such a fool at parties. You're always doing something to draw attention to yourself. When are you going to grow up?"

Now, either he is a fool or not, independently of her comments. He needs to check that reality against her perception. However, he also needs to attend to the message she is sending him about herself. She is saying: "Look, I don't like the way you take center stage at parties because I am not comfortable in the spotlight and become embarrassed." If he responds to her embarrassment rather than to the accusation of his foolishness, he will communicate effectively with her and probably avoid a name-calling, full-blown argument.

Search for Needs Under the Conflict

If a conflict develops and remains stuck, we can assume needs continue not to be met. Under the words of argument lie needs crying for satisfaction. If the words of anger and hurt dominate the conflict, then we need to move the interaction to a different level — to the level of needs.

To do so, we can stop yelling and announce: "Look, we're not getting any place this way. Why don't we take ten minutes alone, try to figure out what we need from each other at this point and then let's get back together and talk about that." You see how the whole process shifts with that kind of intervention. Remember, the basis of almost every interpersonal conflict is unsatisfied needs seeking fulfillment. If ours and the other person's needs are expressed and recognized, they stand a good chance of being filled. In satisfying one another's needs we find practical and concrete ways of saying "I love you" to our friend. Through these loving behaviors, we act in harmony with the energy of love at our heart. Perhaps, then, our most basic need of all is satisfied — the need to live with integrity, to live in love and in union with one another.

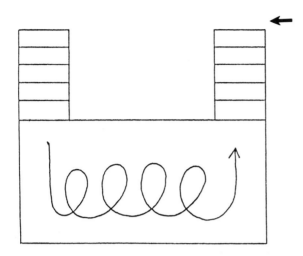

13: FROM THE HEART INTO ENGAGEMENT

If we listen closely to the voice of our heart, we will find ourselves compelled to act in freedom. The drive toward choice moves strongly within us. With choice comes the opportunity to control our own destinies, a position most of us relish. In controlling the flow of our own lives, we make life happen. If we do not make choices we lose control and then life lives upon us. When we live in control of our lives, in freedom, in decision-making stances, then we act according to the energy of freedom that speaks to us from our heart.

Our first parents made choices that have affected all of us throughout the ages. Some of their decisions have been called "original sin." Religions have attempted to explain evil, pain and death by referring to this notion and building theologies and rituals around it.

When I consider the evolutionary process of human life, I find myself pondering the dynamics of human engagement and human denial. Within this context, "original sin" takes on a deeper, fresh meaning. In my imagining, it all may have begun in this fashion:

Some place in the middle, the life process came to a point where highly developed animal forms had emerged. Creatures lived who possessed great physical, sensory and even intellectual skills. Their ability to adapt to their environment and learn new behavior and responses identified them as superior creatures.

As the evolutionary process continued, in an apparently pre-determined way, these animal creatures arrived at a crossing point into a new life form that we would eventually call human. As the intellectual ability of these creatures grew, it reached a point of conscious reflection and choice. Up until now, evolution had progressed solely by the original decisions of its maker; but now it would proceed with the cooperative choices of its own products.

The fundamental choice of these evolving creatures was to advance the evolutionary process of life or to retard it. They would advance created life by choosing humanness, by engaging the dynamics of human life. They would retard life by denying their humanness and choosing to live in a lower state of evolutionary life.

Fortunately for us, they made more choices toward human life. However, some choices led away from humanness. They chose at times to be less than human. These choices, denying human life, became the "original sin." (The word "sin" bothers me because of all its negative connotations. I prefer the word "failings" or "limitations"). These choices denying human life were probably made due to the limited perceptions and judgments about what would enhance human life and what would not. These limited perceptions and judgments, along with the animal drives and instincts of a prior evolutionary state, influenced every human life form to follow.

As a result, today we continue to make choices at times that deny human life. A part of us tends to deny our human power and grace, and seeks to regress to a more primitive life form. These choices of denying human life are the effects of the original choices (sin?) to retard the evolutionary process.

We live today under the mixed influence of our first parents' choices to engage and/or deny human life. We experience surroundings that are truly humanizing and lead to fuller life; and we experience environments that oppress us and turn us away from life. We are touched by forces that aid us in *engaging* life and forces that prompt us to *deny* it.

As we spend time in this world, we gradually develop a general stance as an engager or denier of life. Almost never will you find someone who has totally engaged life or totally denied it. Perhaps Jesus, as presented to us in the scriptures, lived a life in which he completely engaged his full reality as a human person. It has been suggested that persons who commit suicide have totally denied their lives. In one sense that is true. They have completely stopped the evolutionary process at a personal level as far as we know it. However, from another perspective, even their decision to commit suicide may have occurred precisely because they felt trapped without any choices (a truly inhuman position). The decision for suicide at least gave them a choice. In that sense, then, even suicide may possess an element of engagement.

So, the majority of us mix the stances of engagement and denial within us. The stance we take may fluctuate depending on the situation, the people and the time. One day we may feel more engaging; another day we may feel stuck in a denying stance.

As must be evident now, I believe that the personally enriching stance to take in life is that of *Engager*. In so far as we stand in a position of denial, we retard our personal development, and establish a pattern that leads to psychological dysfunctioning and unhappiness.

Throughout the flow of our personal lives, as well as throughout the history of the entire evolutionary process, there lies embedded within all life forms an awesome paradox: we strive to live *forever*; yet we face daily our limitedness and *finitude*. The paradox, especially of human life, is that we reach for infinity and immortality. We possess minds and spirits that grasp for what lies beyond our finiteness. (As I write this, the news is reporting that Voyager X has just passed out of our solar system after an 11 year journey and could continue to exist for billions of years, long after the earth has frozen over or blown to nothingness.)

On the other hand, we have bodies that will slow down, become diseased, decay, rot and pass into oblivion. Thus we see ourselves living forever and ceasing to exist.

According to Ernest Becker, in his Pulitzer Prize winning book, *The Denial of Death*, this contradiction and paradox is so painful to most of us that we repress it, burying it in a myriad of ways. However, no matter how much we try to forget about life and death, the paradox surfaces whenever we face choices in our life. Because within every choice we have, one alternative will lead more fully to life than the other; and at times another option might actually lead to death. The decision to *engage* will always lead to life; the decision to *deny* will lead to death.

Due to the pain involved in the life-death paradox that engulfs us, we attempt to repress or *deny* it. Herein lies our basic stance of denial. We avoid and ignore, from little on, the fact of our death. By doing so, we learn a stance of denial that will affect all our living. Because we deny the fundamental issue of existence, namely nonexistence, we begin to deny a wide variety of life aspects. Since we deny death, we also deny much of life.

We can deny most anything in life: our emotions ("No I am not angry, damn it!"), our sexuality, our behavior, our beliefs, our interpersonal relationships, our creativity, our childlikeness. We can deny our environment, the structures we live and work in; we can deny our families, our histories, our future, our dreams. Every person who comes to see me as a psychotherapist has a major denial going on in his or her life. Neurosis involves the denial of a certain aspect of reality; psychosis, the denial of all reality.

The paranoid person perceives the world and all people as dangerous and threatening, thus denying the reality that at least some people are not dangerous. The hostile person denies another's reality by insisting that the other person should not have acted as, in fact, he or she did act. The anxiety-filled person denies his/her present reality by dramatizing the future.

According to Becker, one of the ways we break the denial stance toward life is to face squarely the harsh reality of our own death. He claims that the Freudian notion of "anality" really means facing "the physical condition of our weakness." He expresses it dramatically:

"Excreting is the curse that threatens madness because it shows man his abject finitude, his physicalness, the likely unreality of his hopes and dreams. But even more immediately, it represents man's utter bafflement at the sheer nonsense of creation: to fashion the sublime miracle of the human face, the mysterium tremendum of radiant feminine beauty, the veritable goddesses that beautiful women are; to bring this out of nothing, out of the void, and make it shine in noonday; to take such a miracle and put miracles again within it, deep in the mystery of eyes that peer out — the eye that gave even the dry Darwin a chill; to do all this, and to combine it with an anus that shits! It is too much. Nature mocks us, and poets live in torture." 33-34

Continuing with the Freudian terminology may help us understand even more clearly the engagement-denial movement in us.

The *oral* stage of development can be understood as a "taking in." We attempt to consume all that is outside of us and make it part of ourself. Psychologically, we see here the struggle to survive, to go on forever. We attempt to become self-sustaining and live fully by the self. In this stage we feel indestructible. If we but take in life, we will live forever.

As the *anal* stage comes upon us, we recognize our physicalness and our serious limitations. We realize we shall die and the self be ended. It is at this point that "Nature mocks us, and poets live in torture."

Next comes the *phallic* stage. Here we attempt to overcome the finiteness of our anal awareness by struggling to survive outside of our limited self. We seek the monuments that will live long after we have decayed and returned to dust. A Spanish saying points out the spirit of this phallic stage: "Every man seeks to have a child, plant a tree and write a book."

Becker suggests that the *Oedipal Project* will then follow. The issue confronted here is: can the child father itself, or will it be fathered by society. In other words, will the person, who strives to live forever, yet recognizes his/her destructibility, take active control of his or her life, or will the person allow him/herself to be pushed and shoved and cajoled through life by the forces outside? When we face the infinity-limitedness of our lives, will we attempt to resolve this tension by actively engaging the life we have, or will we passively, and in depression, allow life to live upon us by denying our ability to partially, at least, father and mother ourselves?

In the Oedipal struggle, then, we attempt to move from dependence to independence, from passivity to activity, and from denial to engagement. We win, in part, the Oedipal Project, when we parent ourselves. We lose the Project when we allow society to parent us, which results in the experience of *castration*. We lose our power, our energies, when we give ourselves over to the forces of society.

The young boy who blindly accepts death in military action suffers castration. The politician who "plays the game" to win is castrated by the machine. The parent always worried about what others think knows castration. Anytime we become faithful to the outside voices when they lack harmony with our inner voice, we experience castration. We lose the Oedipal Project.

Ultimately, the only way to win this awesome project is, in part, by parenting ourselves, and by accepting God in some way as creator-parent. In this way we achieve self-determination here and now, by taking charge of our own lives and living according to our inner energies. By accepting God as creator we attain the hope of overcoming death and living forever. This act of trust involves a "leap of faith" as expressed by Kierkegaard.

Practically, the leap of faith expresses itself in our dynamic movement into our present life. By fully engaging our life and embracing it, we state our belief in the on-goingness of human life. Through engaging our world and self in the here and now, we proclaim our belief in the eternity of human existence and our ultimate victory over death.

The act of engagement, then, is the ultimate act of courage. It springs from the heart. The person is driven by his/her own energies. He/she enters into the fullness of life, risking safety and security in order to live according to his or her own forces. This is the act of health and independence. Engagement is the act that opens the doors to life everlasting.

Characteristics of Engagement and Denial

In his book, *The Heart of Man*, Eric Fromm describes the biophilial and necrophilial persons. These labels correspond somewhat closely to those of Engager and Denier. *Biophilia*, in Greek, means "love of life" and *necrophilia* means "love of death." The Engager loves life and the Denier loves death.

Fromm describes these two kinds of people, which may help us identify our own engaging and denying elements. Please keep in mind as you go through these aspects, we all have some of each. Do not automatically condemn yourself as necrophilial because you notice some of these characteristics in your own life.

1. Focus on present vs. past or future

The Engager lives in the present moment; the Denier dwells in the past or anticipates the future to the exclusion of the present. A woman's teenage daughter was killed in a car accident over 10 years ago. To this day that mother reviews the happenings of that time trying to figure out what she could have done differently to help her child avoid the accident. She denies the present reality of life with a wonderful husband and six other children as she focuses on the past.

Preoccupation with the dentist's appointment next week also constitutes an act of denial of life in the now. I do not want to suggest we spend no time in the future. Most of us enjoy anticipating up-coming events. But when we anticipate events in fear and trepidation, then we will most likely be denying the richness of the present.

2. Focus on positives vs. negatives

We control what we see and how we evaluate it. As I mentioned in Chapter 4 on depression, we have a choice about viewing the positive elements of a situation or centering on the negatives.

A woman in marriage counselling complained that her husband never complimented her. So he began in very small ways. She said: "Well, big deal. Now after 20 years of never hearing a word, he says a couple of dinky little kind things." She denied the positive movement in her husband now, and focused instead on the past 20 years. That denying expression killed off any enthusiasm in the man to continue trying to meet her needs for compliments.

Looking for and focusing on the positive does not mean denying the negative. Certainly, we need to face the entire reality, which often mixes positive and negative. But once the whole is acknowledged, we can then dwell more in the affirmative.

3. Use of love vs. use of force

When we love we embrace another in a freeing way. Our love leads the other out of his or her life, expanding horizons and allowing the other to engage life more fully. Our love also expands our world as we enter the domain of the other.

Force or control, on the other hand, severely limits our lives. It turns us inward in a protective stance. We guard our hearts rather than open our lives. The result is denial and death.

Force or "Law and Order" leads to *fear.* Love leads

to security and safety. None of us can grow in a threatening environment where force creates fear and shuts
down creativity. Children grow into happy, mature
adults when they live in a safe environment. Most of us
remember learning much better from loving caring
teachers who allowed mistakes and experimentation,
then from regimented, controlling instructors.
Love sparks life; force kills the energies of growth in
us and others.

4. Ability to risk vs. the need for certainty
The engaging person risks. He or she does not need
to have every detail figured out before action is taken.
The Denier insists on certainty; and even then hesitates
to act. A manager from the Cadbury Company indicates
that they do not operate on the principle of "Ready, aim,
fire;" but rather "Ready, fire, aim." That captures the
spirit of risk found in the engaging person.
"Let's get on with it" expresses the Engager's
manifesto. Today, the popular expression is "Go for it!"
The Denier sits back and analyzes and checks until every
possible avenue is secured. The Denier's goal in life is to
avoid failure. The Engager sees failure as a way of learning how to succeed.

5. Acceptance vs. Guilt
Engagers know that they are not perfect, nor is the
world. They accept the limitations of daily life — the
flaws, the mistakes and errors that touch us wherever we
journey. Particularly, they do not beat up on themselves
when they face their own weakness.
I worked with a man angry at the world, but most
angry with himself. He made rules for almost every life
event. He reported to me an awful realization he had
while making breakfast one morning: "Dr. Olen, I can't
believe this. But I insist that I make perfect fried eggs. If I
don't, I get very upset with myself. I throw out the eggs
and start over. Can you imagine how many eggs I go
through?"
More often than not, guilt-ridden people create that

ugly feeling because of their high sensitivity to other people's opinions. These people make rules for themselves so they will function perfectly. If they perform without flaw, then other people will think well of them, allowing themselves to then be O.K. with who they are. Naturally, then, when they perform less than perfectly, they fear the negative judgments of others. They feel saddened by the imagined loss of others' esteem; and they feel angry with their poor performance. This combination of sadness and anger create the basis for the feeling we call guilt.

You can see how unfreeing such a dynamic is. Trapped by their own exacting rules and their fear of possible negative reactions from others, Deniers hesitate to enter the rich life chances before them. They tend to deny movement into the unknown, afraid they may fail, thus incurring the negative judgments of others. They stop acting; and take a more defensive position, reacting to what they think will please others. By this stance they deny the energy of their hearts that moves them toward love and freedom.

6. Viewing people as subjects vs. objects

Engagers receive other people with reverence and awe. Persons stand as sacred mysteries, gradually unfolding into higher and richer forms of being. Engagers grasp the goodness of others' essence rather than focus on their social status or functioning.

The Engager looks to enter an I-thou relationship, where through mutual giving and receiving the two become more themselves.

The Denier views other people as objects for his or her use. "How can I gain from this person what I need to enhance me?" is the fundamental question of the denying individual. Focusing on self, the Denier reduces other people to things meant to be manipulated for self-gratification.

People who deny in this fashion are often referred to as narcissistic. They are locked inside of themselves, perceiving themselves as the center of the universe toward which all *things* (including other people) gravitate. Certainly, they cannot grow as persons because the marvelous paradox of living is: we grow as much by giving ourselves to others as by receiving from others. Narcissistic Deniers do not give; they only receive.

7. Letting go vs. holding on

Engagers go through life unencumbered by static perceptions of themselves, others and the world. Just because "It's always been done that way" does not stand in their way of trying a new way. Engagers, for example, read books with the spirit of a student or explorer. They want to know how the writer sees it and feels it. Later on they can assess and judge what they discovered.

In personal relationships, they keep open to entering the other's world more deeply, believing that world will yield ever new dimensions and promises. For instance, marriages between Engagers sparkle with excitement because husband and wife are continually surprised by the other's world. This can only happen between people who keep letting go of the locked in perceptions they had of each other yesterday.

Deniers, on the other hand, see the world today as they have for a hundred yesterdays. If their view of reality worked then, it should still work now. They say, "You hurt my feelings 15 years ago, and you're still trying to hurt me today." No matter how much the other person tries to love them *now*, they can only see through the eyes of yesterday. They literally deny reality today because they insist on clinging to their perceptions of yesterday.

Conditions to Enhance Engagement

Life takes its fullest form in an environment of safety. Consider the gestation of any embryo — the seed finding the security of the damp, quiet earth or the fetus in the protective confines of the mother's womb. Safety is the primary condition for life and growth.

Psychologically, if the small child is safe in her home, she will learn to engage and express her feelings of love and hurt more easily than in a threatening house-hold. Safety is the ground of engagement.

The second condition of engagement is love. Love announces to us that we need not walk into our lives alone. To be loved deeply stimulates our stance toward the love of life. The experience of being loved, I believe, must exist someplace in our history or in our present, to give us the power to engage our lives now. We need not be presently in love to engage life. But we need to know we are lovable because we have been loved.

Justice stands as the third condition for engagement to occur. Remember, justice is the opportunity to exercise our most fundamental right, namely the right to function humanly. When we dwell in structures and relationships that allow us the space and encourage us to act humanly, then we will more easily engage our world.

Finally, the power of freedom needs to surround us if we are to engage rather than deny. In an atmosphere of freedom we are more willing to try out new tasks. My wife, Joelyn and I have begun taking dancing lessons. We both felt very inhibited at the beginning. But because of the sense of freedom and experimentation that pervades the dance studio, we have become much less inhibited and more willing to "let ourselves go." We now can engage the dance.

An atmosphere of freedom gives us the energy to venture and to expand our limited domains. As we do so we fill up our lives with the riches of the entire fabric of humankind.

Cognitive Focusing

If, like me, you recognize some of the characteristics of the Denier to be your own, then you are wondering how to become less a Denier and more an Engager. Perhaps the most effective approach is that of *cognitive focusing*. This term signifies a person's ability to zero in on specific aspects of reality and hold those aspects in his or her range of attention, while excluding other aspects that might interfere with that attention.

We do have power over our thoughts and our attention. Many people believe they do not have such power. Because of that belief, they then do not, in fact, control their attention. The engaging person focuses on lifeful elements; the denying individual attends to death-dealing realities. The choice is ours. We live in a world filled with life and death. We can choose to dwell among the living or among the dead.

The conversion process from Denier to Engager is much like a blind and deaf person opening his eyes and ears and seeing and hearing what is really present in the world, and not what he has been imagining for such a long time. To become an Engager, the denying person gradually learns to see what is really *there*; and not only see it but begin to believe in the reality's life-giving aspects. The Denier begins to realize that the life-giving aspects of the reality are present and able to be activated only by the person himself. In other words, the person brings to the reality life itself.

By engaging the event, we make it become life-giving for us. It is through our mental activity, our cognitive focusing, that we inform any piece of reality with life or death. We literally give life or death to our own experiences and situations.

An example might clarify the point. I enter an airplane and find I am tense and nervous. The plane takes off and I am sweating and afraid until it lands. I have brought to that flight my habit of focusing on the terrible aspects and possibilities of flying. I have informed the event, quite literally, with death — my fear that somehow this machine would not make it and I would die. On the other hand, I enter the plane, sit next to a window and focus on the sense of exhilarating power as the plane races down the runway and lifts off. I then focus on the billowing white clouds and the rich blue sky above us. I relax in the beauty. In this case I have engaged the plane and the flight. Worry is not part of me. I have now informed this same reality with life-giving joy, relaxation and the experience of beauty and power. We give power to what we focus on. Focus on life and we will live; focus on death and we will die.

An Example of Engagement Par Excellence

The scripture story of the dying and rising of Jesus stands out as an example of engagement and its impact on life itself. If original sin involves the choice to deny life in some form, then Jesus stands as the symbol of overcoming "sin" because he did not succumb to denying choices or actions. His life, as presented by the evangelists, speaks of engaging activities from the time he was 12.

Insofar as we deny growth toward fuller life we experience the effects of sin. Death, itself, then, becomes the greatest symbol of the denial of life. Thus, in the scriptures, death symbolizes sin, because theologically sin is an act of denying life.

So along comes Jesus, called to overcome sin or death. How is he to accomplish this awesome task? How is he to overcome that rippling effect of denial created by our first parents?

The answer is clear: Jesus not only engaged the events of his life, but he freely engaged his own death. Christian theology has consistently taught that Jesus chose his death. He walked away from the cliff when the crowd called for his execution because "his time had not yet come."

As I indicated earlier in this chapter, all of us deny our death; we repress the notion of it through much of our lives. Jesus did not deny it. He stood toward it, engaging it. That act of engagement, I believe, captures the true spirit of the resurrection. Jesus entered into death, thus overcoming *denial* as a stance in this world and proclaiming *engagement* as the way of life.

Then he proved his point. He died, passed through death and rose up to the fullness of human life. By engaging death he came to a richer life.

For me the story of the resurrection tells the power of human engagement. If we engage all the aspects of our life, including our death, we too will become whole and free human persons.

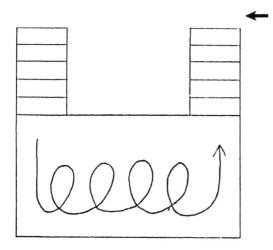

14: FROM THE HEART INTO HAPPINESS

Along with love and freedom, we hear within us the voice that calls us to reach for fullness, satisfaction, contentment, and happiness. Of these three core energies, perhaps happiness eludes us most often. When people ask people if they are happy, so many respond with a shrug of the shoulders and a weak: "I guess so, sure." I wonder if we know that happiness demands certain actions on our part, and a hope that our environment will respond positively to those actions. If I listen well to the voice within, and follow its dictates through my actions, I establish the basis for fulfillment, satisfaction, joy.

Many people search for happiness, but come up short. It eludes them where they seek it; it slips away in the manner of their search. Part of the difficulty in discovering happiness lies in our definition of it. We seek something we do not understand very well. So we end up exploring fantasies of our mind instead of true happiness.

Another part of the difficulty in attaining happiness is our belief that it hides embedded in our environment. We believe happiness would be ours "If I got a raise"; "If she'd say yes"; "If we'd move to a warmer climate"; "If I'd win the Maryland lottery."

In attending to my own life and in working with people struggling to gain happiness, I have noticed *levels* of happiness. There are at least three such levels:

level one = security
level two = integrity
level three = joy

Most people only think of level three (joy) as happiness. They do not understand that security and integrity necessarily precede joy. Consequently, they try to make joy happen without attending first to security and integrity.

How, then, does happiness 3 (joy) come about? On the diagram below (Fig 1) you see the cone shaped figure of the human person. The person lives in an environment (E), which effects the third level of happiness considerably. It takes three elements to create joy and delight: 1) our core or being; 2) our behavior and feelings, or our functioning at the top of the cone; and 3) the response of our environment to our functioning.

Happiness number 1 has to do with our core. When we get in touch with our energies, or our being, we then know who we are. We discover, there, life forces that have existed in us from the beginning. We sense those will continue to exist no matter what happens in our environment. We sense the loving and free movements in us whether we express them in our functioning or not.

When we reach our core we realize our goodness and worth *independently* of how we act or of how other people (our environment) react to us. We experience our goodness simply because we know at our heart these energies of love and freedom make up our being. This realization gives us happiness 1, namely security.

Remember, the realization of who we are at our heart does not give us joy, but it does yield security. We have a sense that who we are cannot be taken from us by others. Nobody can steal from us those energies that make us so valuable. We are loving, free people no matter how our environment responds to us. The energies of our heart are given to us in the act of our

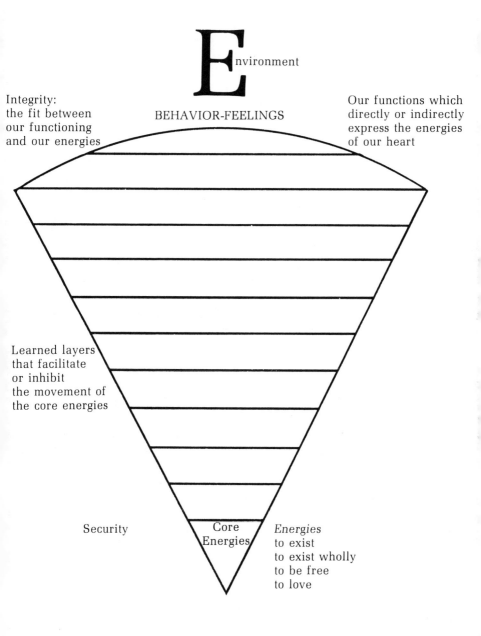

creation. And they will stay with us to our death and hopefully beyond. These energies make us to be rich and beautiful human persons, which no one can alter.

Thus, no matter what we do, or what others do to us, at our heart courses these energies that make us good and worthwhile. In that awareness lies security.

Happiness 2 involves our functioning, that is, how we express our heart's energies in behavior and feelings. When our functioning matches up directly with the energy of our hearts, then we have *integrity*. The fit between our being and doing results in a sense of wholeness and well-being. In effect, our outside matches our inside. We function without any masks, so that what we present in our doing reveals clearly the energies of our heart.

We experience integrity, for example, when the energy of love moves within us and we express that energy in an act of caring for another. We have integrity when the energy of freedom moves us to assertively make our needs known in a restaurant or employer's office.

So, integrity occurs when we sense the fit between our doing and being. But integrity does not necessarily bring us joy.

Happiness 3 or joy results only when the environment responds favorably to our functioning. When we gain a three-way fit among our core energies, our functioning and the environment, then we know joy.

Let's say a man senses the energy of freedom in himself pushing him toward a different function in the company. He senses the freedom this move would bring and knows the energy within him is good and right. He now has *security*. He knows his goodness independently of what he does or how his boss will respond.

Next, he goes to his boss and expresses his desire to move to another position. He functions according to his being. He experiences the fit within himself, and now has *integrity*. He is whole.

Joy occurs or does not occur depending on the

response of his environment. If his boss says "no," the employee will have security and integrity, but little joy; if his boss says "yes," then the employee has the three-way fit (functions match being, and environment matches functions) that yields joy. It is this joy that most of us think of when we seek happiness.

As you can realize we only control our integrity. We do not have too much control over our joy. Our security is given. We only have to discover it. We do not create our energies or our goodness. We only need to recognize them.

We do, however, have control and power over our behavior and our feelings. Consequently, *we* create our own sense of integrity by striving to match our functions to our energies. In this area we can always improve, becoming more and more integral.

We can have some control over our environment, trying to get it to match our functioning. But we cannot expect to totally dominate and manipulate the environment to respond perfectly to us.

In friendship or marriage, for example, we attempt to influence our partner so that he or she will respond to us in ways that will bring us joy. However, the other person also possesses freedom to respond in a fitting way or not.

Some people struggle for joy by focusing on the environment, trying to manipulate it to yield aspects that will bring delight. If they do this without consideration of their own integrity (which involves awareness of their heart), they will experience momentary delight, but not sustained joy that results in peace.

In some respects then, joy is out of our control. The environment needs to respond favorably to our integral functioning for us to know joy. We control our integrity. We can act faithfully to our heart. We can seek integrity directly. But we cannot achieve real joy unless the environment cooperates with our integral functioning.

The bible prophet Jeremiah offers an excellent example of integrity without much joy. The voice of God was "like a roaring lion" within him. This was the energy of his heart. He could not contain it. It exploded up through his layers. He had to function. So he preached the word of God. Thus he had integrity. His outside behavior matched the energy of his heart.

But his audiences did not appreciate his message of repentance and conversion. They rejected him and tried to persecute him. He did not have joy, since his environment reacted so negatively.

But he did have his integrity, happiness number 2. And in the circumstances, that was the best he could do. He was in charge of his integrity. He could only hope for his environment to yield joy by cooperating with his functioning.

As pursuers of joy, then, we need to focus on our integrity. We control that almost totally. Joy is frosting on the cake. What a delightful surprise when the environment matches up with our integral behavior. Had his listeners given him standing ovations, and then repented, Jeremiah would have known real joy. But he could not control the crowd's response, and had to remain satisfied with his own integrity.

We have been looking at happiness from the point of view of the one seeking it. We need to briefly consider those many times when *we* are the environment for someone else seeking joy. In many circumstances we are able to respond to people in such a way as to bring them joy.

If my wife tells me of her love for me, and I respond with an off-the-cuff, "That's nice," I probably do not give her joy. If, however, I take her in my arms and tell her I love her too, then I, as her environment, respond fittingly to her.

One of the beauties of marriage is precisely my ability to know the needs of my partner and to respond to her in caring ways. I become for my wife, then, literally a *source of joy.* If we are sensitive environments to others, we will be for them gifts of joy and delight.

One of the reasons why counselors can help people

is that they try to set a receptive and caring environment for people to express the depths of their hearts. To receive well someone who wants to give of him or herself is truly a gift. When the process of communication works well, the Giver expresses through behavior and feelings a message that rises from the heart (integrity). When the message is received by some significant part of the environment, the Giver experiences a sense of fit and a personal fulfillment in the completion of the exchange (joy).

Oftentimes, by creating a responsive environment for others, we can aid them in living with more integrity. For example, as parents we try to create an environment that matches and magnifies the voice of our children's hearts. By our living with love and freedom, we can help our children know the energies of love and freedom within themselves. By getting in touch with those energies, they can then learn to function directly out of them. They learn integrity by hearing the voice of their hearts in their environment.

Joy, then, comes in large part from our environment as a gift to us. We create the basis for joy by our efforts to live with integrity, trying to match our behavior and feelings to the energies of our heart. As environments for others, we give joy by sensitively and lovingly responding to their integral functioning. In fact, we magnify the voice of love and freedom that whispers in their hearts.

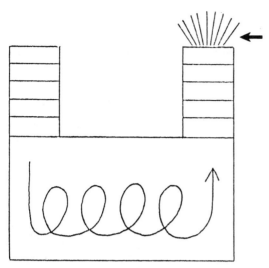

15: VOICES THAT SPEAK FOREVER

Having attempted to listen well to my own heart over the years, and having listened to the hearts of many other people in counselling, questions arise in me: Will these voices ever stop, or will they go on speaking forever? Do the voices die when the body fails? Do the voices ever really explain the meaning and purpose of human life and death? Why do we discover in us energies of love, freedom and fulfillment? What are their ultimate purpose?

Much of philosophy and religion has been created in order to deal with the awesome questions regarding the meaning of life and the reality of death. All of us try to find some answers to these troubling questions. Throughout the ages, people have attempted to respond to the questions, some with great simplicity and others through complex systems of thought, myth and, perhaps, some magic.

For each of us the big question is: What happens to us after death? We all try answering that question in different ways according to our life circumstances. As a child I believed that if I lived a good life, I would go to heaven after death. And heaven was a place in the sky where I could sit and eat all the bananas I wanted without getting sick. As the years went on and I did not enjoy bananas as much as I enjoyed other people, my notion of heaven changed to a place where I could be with all my friends playing sports.

Most of us see a process of evolution in our way of thinking of life after death. For all of us there remains an area of doubt about any existence after death. We simply cannot be sure. But most of us try to believe (and we hope) that we do not end with our death.

I want to conclude this book about the U process and the voices of our heart with a reflection on the flow of life and death. What I present here is simply a speculation that presently makes sense to me. It is my way of trying to answer the question of what happens after death. I offer it, not as a religion or a philosophy, but as a personal reflection for you to use as a stimulant to your own thoughts on life and death.

First of all, I believe death will not end our personal existence. All of us try to find some "proof" for our continued life after death. Although I have studied St. Thomas Aquinas and many other philosophers and theologians, the most compelling "proof" of my continued existence comes from my personal experience of love. It seems to me that the characteristic of *foreverness* is contained in the act of loving. When we love someone, we love them forever at the moment of loving. Certainly, this does not mean we cannot stop loving someone. Because we live in the dimension of time almost everything can change.

But in the act of loving itself, we experience a forever quality, a longing to hold the moment. In fact, within the act of loving we often experience the transcendence of time. I experience my love for my wife, children and parents as a forever love, a love that cries out to continue without end.

This awareness of love as forever forces me to believe that the characteristic of foreverness will, in fact, be satisfied. If *forever* is built right into the very nature of loving, then it will be fulfilled as part of the completion of our nature as loving (and therefore eternal) beings. Because we love, and love yearns to be forever, we will live forever.

If we are to live forever, then how are we to fill up the space and time? To answer that question from a philosophical point of view, we might simply respond: This may be a non-question because in our next state of existence we may not even have the dimensions of space and time.

However, because we think in terms of space and time, it helps to think of our foreverness in those terms. First, let's look to how we perhaps did fill up space and time; and then we can consider how we might in the future.

I used to believe I came into existence first around 1940 when my dad and mom mixed a sperm and ovum and God intervened with the critical act of creation, thus giving me existence for the first time. Over the years I have heard and read many theories of how life began that have led me to wonder what more might have gone into my making.

I wonder, for instance, what *other* life forces came together to form me as this human person. Rather than think, as some Re-incarnationists do, that I evolved directly from a monkey, or snake or flower, I speculate that many life forces or other existences came together to make me who I am. If we generally suggest three life forces came together — Dad, Mom, and God — why not seven or 777? Perhaps the life energies of certain animals, plants, and other people converged in a single instant with my dad and mom and God to form me as this unique human creature.

We may not have conscious awareness of our prior states of being, not because they did not exist, but only because our level of consciousness presently is not able to re-capture those prior times. Certainly this line of thinking would add some strength to those arguments suggesting we are different by nature from one another, not only by nurture and environment.

The point here is simply that the root of our present

existence may extend backwards to the very beginnings of life (if, in fact, there even was a beginning). Sensing that we have existed in various configurations of life forms from the beginning, may make it easier to understand the meaning and process of our future. If we have always existed in some life forms, then it is more likely that we will continue to exist in new and more exciting life forms in the future.

Up until this present life form, our consciousness has been severely limited. We have not been very aware of ourselves, our past or future. As human persons, we have reached a new and exciting stage of awareness. We can think reflectively on our beginnings and endings. But even our consciousness appears weak and minimal. Our memory of the past fades with passing years. We cannot hold in consciousness all the life forces that have touched us since we have been in human form. We still remain, it appears, at the lower end of our evolutionary movement toward full consciousness and existence.

Then, what is yet to come? Simply put, the *continuation of consciousness.* I believe that life after death will involve greater levels of awareness and the continued development of powers we now possess in very limited ways. Perhaps we will possess a greater sense of our roots, of those life forces that make us who we are. Perhaps we will know consciously all who we are united to in love and power. Perhaps, through consciousness, we will experience personal freedom we now only vaguely touch.

More specifically, when we make the transition into the next level of awareness (pass from this life into death and then whatever lies beyond), I believe we will experience consciously the foreverness of our love. For example, now I experience a certain eternal quality in my love for Joelyn, my wife. I have a sense of loving her forever; but that sense is limited by unawareness of who I am fully, or who she is fully or of what will happen 15 years from now, or of what happens when we both die. In other words, I sense that foreverness of our bonding in very hazy ways.

In our next life state, I believe I will *know* the fore-verness of our loving relationship. I will be bonded to Joelyn and she to me in a love that began in this life (per-haps even in prior life states!) and now will become ever more intense and truly last forever.

If I should die before her, and enter into this aware-ness and intensity of loving her, I will be wholly satis-fied, for she will be present to me. She, however, will grieve my loss and suffer temporarily only because in her limited awareness and experience she will not sense our eternal bondedness as I know it. When she makes her transition through death, then she too will know what all the decreased know, namely we are bonded forever to all we love.

I like to believe that in our next life we will simply know consciously all the loving bonds we have formed here, and expand those in intensity and in number. As we pass into our next (but certainly not last) form of being, we will know, not only the increase of our loving, but also the fuller experience of personal freedom. Be-cause of our new awareness of ourselves and of life around us, our choices for growth will increase, as will our wisdom in making choices for good.

As we choose growth and act through conscious lov-ing, we will be joining our life force to that of others. The possibility of forming new creations becomes endless. Most of us, at least in the West, hope to protect our in-dividuality, thus we tend to reject any loss of ourselves in some kind of "cosmic whole." But if we could have both, our individuality and a sense of union with other life forms to create a new existence, we might indeed know the best of both worlds.

We have signs even in this life of such a process, namely maintaining our personal uniqueness and be-coming a new creation as we join life forces with others. Marriage and family give us a hint of future possibilities. I have, at times, yearned to be so one with my wife that the boundaries of my individuality seemed to fade and we became a new creation. Nonetheless, we both remained our own selves. Then came the joining of our life forces to give life to our children, Andy and Amy. At times, in family life, (and not always happily so) we seem to lose our boundaries as parents as our children make their many demands on us. At other moments, we feel blended and bonded so intimately with our families that we believe and know we are more than ourselves.

When, in our next life form, we join together with all those we love, and with our increased bonding and awareness of God or some transcendent power, there is no telling what might result. I think we can know, however, it will be very good. St. Paul apparently had some momentary expanded consciousness, and knew it to be good. He could not express it to us because of his limitations in sharing it and our limitations in receiving it.

What we take into life after death will, I think, depend on how humanly we live in this life. The more we grow in love, freedom and consciousness here, the richer soil we will bring into our next level of conscious living. How we communicate and bond with people here, how we love others, how we make choices, how we engage life will, I believe, determine the level of existence we will attain in the next step of our eternal process toward fullness.

Perhaps a major difference between then and now will be our ability to hear the voice of our heart. What presently sounds faint and distant will then resound in our spirit, fill us, and find expression in loving and free responses. The voices of other hearts, speaking the same language, will magnify the sound we hear within. And all the whispers of all our hearts will join together and reverberate with great power throughout the universe forever and ever.

Sponsor a *DALE OLEN* WORKSHOP

Dale Olen would be happy to present a lecture on the various topics presented in this book to your group or organization. Chapters 7-11, especially, provide many excellent lecture and workshop opportunities.

☐ Yes, I am interested in more information about a DALE OLEN WORKSHOP.

NAME _____

ORGANIZATION _____

ADDRESS _____

CITY _____ STATE_____ ZIP _____

PHONE _____

Return this form to:

Life Skills Center
10012 W. Capitol Drive
Milwaukee, WI 53222